NONDUALITY AND MIND-ONLY

THROUGH THE PRISM OF REALITY

L. Ron Gardner

VERNAL POINT
PUBLISHING

Books by L. Ron Gardner

Beyond the Power of Now: A Guide to, and Beyond, Eckhart Tolle's Teachings

Electrical Christianity: A Revolutionary Guide to Jesus' Teachings and Spiritual Enlightenment

Kill Jesus: The Shocking Return of the Chosen One

Buddhist Book Reviews for Smarties

Zen Mind, Thinker's Mind: New Perspectives on Buddhadharma, Consciousness, and Awakening

Radical Dzogchen: The Direct Way to En-Light-enment

Nonduality and Mind-Only through the Prism of Reality

CONTENTS

LIST OF DIAGRAMS

Introduction

The Story of This Book

After completing and publishing *Zen Mind, Thinker's Mind* and *Radical Dzogchen* in 2022, I decided that my next writing project would be a Kabbalah book. While beginning work on it, I found myself spending my free time watching YouTube videos on nonduality and Mind (or Consciousness)-Only idealism. This inspired me to read some contemporary books on these subjects. In short, neither the books nor the YouTube videos impressed me; so I decided to put my Kabbalah book on hold and first write *Nonduality and Mind-Only through the Prism of Reality*.

Because the Mind-Only idealism that I subscribe to involves explaining emanation and creation, I knew that I'd be able to integrate my seminal Kabbalistic insights into my thesis and paradigm, effectively killing two birds with one stone. I also knew that by adding Kashmir Shaivism metaphysics and Hegelian phenomenology of Spirit to my paradigm, I would be able to provide a unique and profound description of the "prismatic" intermundia between unmanifest Mind, the Supreme Source (of emanation and creation), and the terrestrial world we humans inhabit.

I also knew that engaging my sharpest students in discussions on nonduality and Mind-Only would not only lead me to new insights on the subject matter (which it especially did regarding the Kabbalistic Tree of Life), but also provide an agreeable Socratic format for the book. I've freely edited and added to my exchanges with my students in order to provide pithy and provocative dialogue that I think most readers will find worthy of serious contemplation.

Unlike most spiritual writers, I'm not the least shy about professing and promoting what I consider to be right spiritual politics. And given the current uber-polarized political climate, I felt it was apropos to extend the quasi-Hegelian phenomenology of Spirit analysis that I employ throughout my book into a consideration of the recent and present sociopolitical and sociocultural zeitgeist. Although the zeitgeist is always changing, the arguments I make for right spiritual politics are not; they are perennial and always hold true, cohering with dualistic man's nature in a nondual universe.

Now, a forewarning to those averse to open controversy, blatant irreverence, acidic criticism of others, and political incorrectness: My writings are teeming with them. My mantra is: "Dale Carnegie I ain't." My modus operandi, a la Howard Cosell, is: "I just tell it like it is (or how I perceive it), and let the chips fall where they may." So prepare yourself for the unrepentant "blasphemy" you are about to encounter in this book.

Summary of This Book

The book consists of sixteen chapters, which I'll now summarize:

Chapter 1. "Nonduality and Mind-Only": Explains what nonduality, Mind, and Mind-Only mean, providing the first "base" for the book to build upon.

Chapter 2. "Reality and reality": Differentiates Ultimate (unmanifest, spaceless-timeless) Reality from phenomenal (manifest, space-time) reality, providing the second "base" for the book to build upon.

Chapter 3. "Huang Po and the One Mind": Presents Zen master Huang Po's Dharma to illustrate reductive Mind-Only teachings that don't explain the "bridge" between Ultimate Reality (Mind) and phenomenal reality (*Maya*).

Chapter 4. "The *Lankavatara Sutra* and the One Mind": Elaborates the *Lankavatara Sutra*, the foremost Yogacara text, as a veiled doctrine of Divine Descent of Mind (*Dharmamegha*) into yogis (*bodhisattvas*), and properly explains reality as a manifestation of (universal) Mind rather than a projection of the (individual) mind.

Chapter 5. "Kashmir Shaivism: The Involution of Ultimate Reality": Elaborates the 36-*tattva* (constituent-principle) system of Kashmir Shaivism (KS), which "maps" how Mind (or *Siva*), as uncontracted Consciousness-Energy (*Siva-Shakti*), "plans" and then "rolls out" the universe as *Maya* (contracted *Siva-Shakti*), which veils the recognition of Mind (or *Siva*) from embodied beings (*samsarins*), who must, through the practice of yoga, seek to regain their Divine status as immanent, uncontracted *Siva*.

Chapter 6. "The Perversion of Kashmir Shaivism's Mind-Only Doctrine": Critiques Christopher Wallis's KS teachings, reviews his book *The Recognition Sutras*, and finds Wallis, perhaps the most popular Western teacher of tantra and KS, guilty of the perversion of Kashmir Shaivism—especially its Mind (or Consciousness)-Only doctrine. Sadhguru is also identified as guilty of tantric Shaivism perversion.

Chapter 7. "Kabbalah: Descent of the Divine through the Four Worlds": Reviews/critiques canonical Kabbalah/Qabalah books and teachings, rejecting them as satisfactory descriptions/explanations of the theosophical Kabbalah and the Tree of Life. A seminal new Tree-of-Life theosophy is then presented that explains the relationship (including the cosmological history) between Mind (Creator) and manifestation (creation).

Chapter 8. "Beyond *The Phenomenology of Spirit*, Part 1": Explains Hegelian idealism and dialectic, briefly considering them in the contexts of epistemology, spirituality, Marxism, and sociopolitics.

Chapter 9. "The Prismatic Paradigm, Part 1": Introduces my "Prismatic Paradigm," which creatively combines Kashmir Shaivism, Kabbalah, and phenomenology of Spirit to construct a new Kabbalistic Tree of Life, which, as an integral Mind/manifestation schema, views creation as a refractive theophany. The focus of this discussion is mainly on Kashmir Shaivism in relation to the Prismatic Paradigm.

Chapter 10. "The Prismatic Paradigm, Part 2": Continues my consideration of the Prismatic Paradigm, with the focus mainly on the Tree of Life and astrology.

Chapter 11. "Beyond *The Phenomenology of Spirit*, Part 2": Continues my consideration of the phenomenology of Spirit as it pertains to sociopolitics. The "Dialectical Sociopolitical Wheel" is introduced as a sphere in my new Kabbalistic Tree of Life, and the two pertinent dialectical oppositions—capitalism vs. socialism and individualism vs. statism—are considered, along with the sociopolitics of Ken Wilber, Adi Da Samraj, and Klaus Schwab.

Chapter 12. "Beyond *The Phenomenology of Spirit*, Part 3": Introduces the "Dialectical Sociocultural Wheel" as a sphere in my new Kabbalistic Tree of Life, and designates self-identity/self-expression versus relationships/partnerships as its horizontal axis and home/family versus livelihood/life mission as its vertical axis. The focus in this chapter is on the horizontal axis and its subversion by cultural Marxism.

Chapter 13. "Beyond *The Phenomenology of Spirit*, Part 4": Elaborates the vertical axis of the Dialectical Sociocultural Wheel and explains how, in the current zeitgeist, the dialectic of home/family versus livelihood/life mission is, like the horizontal axis of self-identity/self-expression versus relationships/partnerships, being subverted by cultural Marxism.

Chapter 14. "Present-Day Nonduality and Mind-Only Teachings": Critiques the words/works of prominent nonduality/Mind-Only authors Robert Wolfe, Rupert Spira, Bernardo Kastrup, Donald Hoffman, Jay Michaelson, and David Loy, exposing them as wisdom-deficient and disintegral.

Chapter 15. "Top-Down Monistic Idealism/Bottom-Up Dualistic Realism": Summarizes my idealist view as "top-down monistic idealism/bottom-up dualistic realism," which contends that universal, spaceless-timeless Mind (or Consciousness), the Real, has become everything, the totality of space-time existents; and once Mind, via its inseparable *Shakti*, "rolls out" the universe of existents, then duality—meaning separate space-time entities and consequent subject-object relations—ensues, and this manifest, dualistic reality is real, not an illusion, because nothing unreal can come from the Real.

Chapter 16. "Power-of-Now Meditation (Holy Communion)": Provides Power-of-Now Meditation/Divine (or Holy) Communion instructions that explain how to access the timeless Now (or Divine Presence) and receive (or conduct) its en-Light-ening Energy (or divinizing Power), and thereby experience the Spirit-full Reality of Mind-Only nonduality. Excerpts from my book *Electrical Christianity* ("The Practice of True Holy Communion," "Ohm's Law and Spiritual Energy," and "Ohm's Law and the Eucharist") apply Ohm's Law and Hegelian dialectic to explain the "mechanics" of

spiritual en-Light-enment; and pertinent Kabbalah and Kashmir Shaivism writings provide further light on Divine (or
Holy) Communion and Divine (Power-of-Now) Reception.

Because this book contains considerable Buddhist, Hindu, and
Kabbalistic terminology, I have included an extensive glossary.
As with my previous nonfiction books, I have included my Spir-
itual Reading List, which I've upgraded with new additions.

Every book I write aims to break seminal new ground in the
spiritual tradition or topic it covers—sans this aim, I wouldn't
be a spiritual writer. It is my hope that readers will find my goal
successful with this book.

Notes to the Reader

Except for a handful of terms that have entered the common lexicon (such as yoga, tantra, and guru), I have generally, but not in all cases, italicized Buddhist, Hindu yogic, and Kabbalistic terms. One of the toughest tasks in writing spiritual books is deciding which terms to capitalize, and when. For example, a term such as "Power" might merit capitalization in one context, but not another. The calls regarding italicization and capitalization were often subjective, and if I ever do a second edition, I'll doubtless end up changing some of them.

In reading this book, you'll see that I sometimes capitalize "En-Light-enment," and sometimes don't. In general (though not always), when you see "En-Light-enment" (or "Enlightenment"), I am referring to full or final spiritual Awakening, and when you see "en-Light-enment," I am signifying the process of Awakening via Light-Energy. In borderline cases, where the term could apply to both the process of Awakening and final Awakening, I made a subjective call based on the context in which the term is used.

This book is composed mainly in a question-and-answer format, with the questions and answers derived principally from discussions with a couple of my students. I have freely edited the questions and answers so as to provide readers with the most enlightening information and instruction. To this end, I have, when pertinent, interjected material from my previous books and other sources into the dialogues.

CHAPTER ONE

Nonduality and Mind-Only

What is Nonduality?

From my perspective, and that of the foremost spiritual traditions, there is only one true version of nonduality—that of a single uncreated, unmanifest Mind, or Being-Consciousness, or Divine Existent, as the Source, Substance, Condition, and Reality of reality (meaning the totality of manifest existents). In other words, nonduality, as I and the foremost spiritual traditions define it, means Mind-Only, which means that this One Mind, or Being-Consciousness, has become everything; yet, paradoxically, because it is forever unmanifest, and thus outside time and space, it has not become anything.

What can you say about this Mind?

Because Mind (or Consciousness), the single Reality, transcendentally (or timelessly and spacelessly) alone exists, it is Self-Existing as Supreme (or Divine) Being; hence, it isn't just Consciousness, but Being-Consciousness. Moreover, because Mind is Divine (or Di-"vine"), it consists not only of the "vine" of Consciousness (or Awareness), but also the "vine" of Energy (or Spirit); hence, it isn't just Being-Consciousness, but Being-Consciousness-Energy. In other words, Mind is Self-Existing, Self-Radiating Self-Awareness, the Di-"vine" Existent that has become all existents.

When, in our discussions, we focus on uncreated Mind as Creator (or Creator God), we'll consider specifics regarding its "action" in, and as, *Maya* (phenomenal reality, which has been "measured out" from the Immeasurable, meaning Mind). And the final chapter of the book [Chapter Sixteen] will provide specifics on the way to yogically coincide with Mind, the Divine Existent, by receiving its en-Light-ening "action," *Shakti*, a.k.a. the Holy Spirit and the true Power of Now.

Why Did Mind Become Everything?

No one knows why Mind (a.k.a. God, Allah, Brahman, *Samantabhadra*, *Siva*, et al.) emanated the universe of existents. Per Kashmir Shaivism, the most esoteric Hindu yoga tradition, the answer is "because *Siva* willed it." And the result is the universe as the "Dance of *Siva*," with *Siva* as the "Lord of the Dance," the Conductor of His Divine Play in, and as, *Maya*.

How did Mind Become Everything?

It is impossible for us humans to know how Mind, the ineffable "Mental Substance" of the "Holy One," the "All-Creating Monarch," has become all energies, inanimate matter, and living organisms. Nonetheless, a couple of esoteric spiritual traditions—Kashmir Shaivism and Kabbalah—which we'll focus on in our discussions, have provided us with revelatory "maps" or top-down schemas that, to a degree, explain the hierarchical descent of Mind, the Absolute, into the gradient planes of the relative. Moreover, other teachings, which we'll also examine, have likewise provided us with worthwhile material regarding unmanifest Mind and its relation to manifest existence.

CHAPTER TWO

Reality and reality

So, from your perspective, Mind is uncreated Ultimate Reality, and all that has manifested from Mind, meaning the universe of created existents, constitutes phenomenal reality?

Yes. Whatever is created is ultimately destroyed, and that describes phenomenal reality, a.k.a. *Maya*.

The fact that all created "things" are not Ultimate Reality has led many (including big-name physicists and philosophers) to conclude that Ultimate Reality must therefore be Nothing or Nothingness. But that is untenable, because something cannot come from nothing. Those who subscribe to the *ex-nihilo* hypothesis are guilty of what Ayn Rand calls the "reification of zero," the faulty attribution of ontological status to a non-existent. Mind is formless, spaceless, and timeless, but it is not Nothingness or Emptiness. Rather, it is an ineffable, omnipresent "Consciousness" or "Mental Substance"—the uncreated "Thing"-in-Itself. And because this Mind, or Intelligent Awareness, is, per Tibetan Dzogchen, the "All-Creating Monarch," as well as the acausal Absolute, it is an apt synonym for "God."

Adyashanti, the popular Advaita guru, says, "Before consciousness there is emptiness. Emptiness is the ultimate principle, the Self—the source of all. That awareness of consciousness is emptiness."

Adyashanti is a deluded "guru" sans a philosophic clue. His spiel is combining Madhyamaka/Zen blather with surface-level Advaita

Vedanta. And the product of this "marriage" is nothing short of a metaphysics disaster. His cluelessness is so severe that he absurdly describes Enlightenment as "emptiness looking at emptiness."

Again, emptiness is a non-existent with no ontological status. There can be no "emptiness," or lack of content, without some thing (such as a pocket) or Being (such as God/Mind) to be devoid of form. Consciousness is not emptiness but is full of radiant Light-Energy. It is formless, but not formlessness or emptiness. Emptiness (the absence of content or forms) can only be an object to the Subject/Seer—Being-Consciousness/ Self-Existing Awareness—the Ultimate Principle. Finally, the idea that Consciousness/consciousness and life could some-how emerge from an inert void is untenable, because, again, something cannot come from nothing.

Some Buddhist and Hindu philosophies describe the ontological status of existents in Maya *as "neither existing nor non-existing." What can you say about this?*

Saying that phenomenal existents neither exist nor don't exist is another way of saying they appear in *Maya* but lack self-ex-istence because their ontological status is that of a manifes-tation of the Single Existent, the One Mind. I consider these teachings guilty of truth-muddling and sophistry, because a clear, straight-forward spiritual teaching would describe the ontological status of existents the way I do.

I'm clear on your designation of Mind, or Being-Consciousness, as Ultimate Reality, but not on your definition of phenomenal reality, which some say is an illusion.

Whatever exists is real, whatever doesn't exist is unreal. Dreams, imaginations, and "illusions" are real, simply be-cause they exist, or appear, in phenomenal reality; but their ontological status must be differentiated from that of more substantial existents.

So, to be clear, in our series of discussions, what we're going to be considering is the interface between Ultimate Reality, or unmanifest Mind, and phenomenal reality, that which manifests from Mind. And because Mind subsumes all that manifests from it, our discussions will necessarily entail the subject of nonduality.

Correct. And when I compile our talks into a book, I'm going to title it *Nonduality and Mind-Only through the Prism of Reality.*

CHAPTER THREE

Huang Po and the One Mind

In your book Zen Mind, Thinker's Mind*, you devote two chapters to Zen master Huang Po's teachings. What can you say about his nonduality and Mind-Only teachings as they pertain to what you call the "prism of reality"?*

I'm a huge fan of Huang Po (died 850 AD), my favorite Zen master. And I highly recommend the book *The Zen Teaching of Huang Po* by John Blofeld. That said, I think it's also important to do what Huang Po fails to do: consider his radical nonduality and Mind-Only teachings from the viewpoint of beings enmeshed in *Maya*. Here [below], for us to consider, are a few excerpts from *The Zen Teaching of Huang Po* that summarize his view on nonduality and the One Mind:

> The Master said to me: All the Buddhas and all sentient beings are nothing but the One Mind, beside which nothing exists. This Mind, which is without beginning, is unborn and indestructible. It is like the boundless void which cannot be fathomed or measured.

> Only awake to the One Mind and there is nothing whatsoever to be attained. This is the real Buddha. The Buddha and all sentient beings are the One Mind and nothing else.

> The One Mind alone is the Buddha, and there is no distinction between the Buddha and sentient things, but that sentient beings are attached to forms and so seek externally for Buddhahood. By their very seeking they lose it, for that

is using the Buddha to seek for the Buddha and using mind
to grasp Mind.

There has never been a single thing; then where's defiling
dust to cling? If you can understand the heart of this, why
talk of transcendental bliss?

In short, Huang Po says there is only "the One Mind, beside
which nothing exists"; therefore, "there has never been a single
thing." In other words, all "things" are just temporary modifica-
tions or permutations of the "Thing-in-Itself," the Absolute, or
Mind, which has become all things. Moreover, "the Buddha,"
meaning one's immanent Buddha-nature, or True Self, likewise is not a "thing," but the One Mind.

So, there is only one Truth?

Again, as Huang Po puts it, "There has never been a single thing...
There is only the One Mind, beside which nothing exists." But
although all existents are just forms of the single Existent, or
Being-Consciousness, for us to function in the "real," or conditional, world, we, as conditional beings, must also acknowledge
the truth (or reality) of its laws, distinctions, and boundaries.

*But if there is only the One Mind, or Being-Consciousness, which has
become everything, doesn't that negate individual identity and result
in the same nihilism as Nagarjuna's Madhyamaka?*

No. Once the One Mind, or "God," emanates the universe of existents from Itself, creating the phenomenal worlds, a.k.a. *Maya*,
these existents are endowed with individual identities. Moreover,
the One Mind, or "God," has blessed man with the cognitive ability to identify, and thus differentiate, these existents.

So in *Maya*, that which has been "measured out" from the
Immeasurable, a.k.a. "God," or Mind, individual things and

beings are a reality; but from the viewpoint of the Absolute, there has "never been a single thing" because all "things" are just temporary manifestations of the "Thing Itself," the One Mind, or Being-Consciousness.

Because Zen doesn't account for procession of the One to the Many, but simply reduces the Many to the One, its nonduality can be characterized as one-dimensional, as less than integral.

Why do you think Huang Po and his fellow Zen masters fail to consider the gradient "prism of reality," the Absolute as refracted through the emanated hierarchical dimensions of manifest existence?

Because Zen is a reductive, tunnel-vision tradition that eschews metaphysics. And because of this, it can't account for and explain the Tree of Life, meaning the intermediary constitutive agencies and principles that link "Heaven" (the immaterial Absolute) to "Earth" (the material relative). As such, Zen can be categorized as "digital spirituality," whereas traditions such as Kabbalah and Kashmir Shaivism can be classified as "analog spirituality," because, in contrast to Zen, they attempt to account for the emanated "interface" of dimensions and elements that links "Heaven" and "Earth."

Those interested in a deeper and wider consideration of Zen's metaphysical limitations, and the reasons for them, should refer to my book *Zen Mind, Thinker's Mind: New Perspectives on Buddhadharma, Consciousness, and Awakening*, wherein I argue that Zen's allegiance to Madhyamaka philosophy and failure to account for the *Trikaya* (*Dharmakaya*, *Sambhogakaya*, *Nirmanakaya*), the Buddhist Trinity, circumscribed its metaphysical development.

CHAPTER FOUR

The *Lankavatara Sutra* and the One Mind

What can you say about the Lankavatara Sutra *and the One Mind?*

The *Lankavatara Sutra* (abbreviated LS *or Lanka*) is perhaps the most profound and important Mahayana Buddhist sutra. In contrast to Nagarjuna's Madhyamaka doctrine, it (via its Yogacara Cittamatra philosophy) asserts that Mind, not emptiness, is the Essence of all phenomena. Moreover, whereas Madhyamaka does not posit an Ultimate Reality but merely equates all existents, or forms, with emptiness, the *Lanka* identifies this single, universal Mind, or Consciousness, as Ultimate Reality, and maintains that It has become everything. As such, the LS is akin to Hindu Kashmir Shaivism, Tibetan Dzogchen, and the Zen of Mind-Only masters, such as Huang Po.

What's especially interesting regarding the LS is that it not only identifies Mind as Ultimate Reality, but also, metaphorically, describes Its enlightening action as a "Descent into Lanka," meaning a plunging into the *Tathagatagarbha* (the Heart-cave, or "womb of Buddhahood"), wherein yogis (*bodhisattvas*) are "reborn" as, or "converted" into, Buddhas. Since, in my book *Zen Mind, Thinker's Mind*, I describe this "Descent into Lanka" in detail, I'll here simply repeat what I wrote, which identifies the *Lanka* as a veiled *Shaktipat* (or Divine-descent) doctrine.

Descent into Lanka

To the spiritual cognoscenti, it is clear that the LS is about the descent of the Divine (as the *Dharmamegha*, or "Dharma Cloud") into the *Tathagatagarba* (or Heart-cave), which precipitates full En-lightenment, or *Bodhicitta*. The term "Lankavatara" means "descent into Lanka," and Lanka (a solitary, or sacred, "island"), like Sri (meaning "Holy") Lanka, is a metaphor for the *Tathagatagarbha*, the "place," or "locus," or "womb," where one is "reborn" as a Buddha. In the Hindu *Yoga Sutras*, reaching this "island," (a.k.a. *Hridayam*, or Heart-center) is termed *kaivalya*, which means "isolation" from the defilements that, in Yogacara terms, taint the seven forms of con-sciousness that precede the en-Light-ening eighth one, *Alaya-vi-jnana*. Yogacara means "the practice of yoga," and the highest yoga, Di-"vine" yoga, is the union of the "vine" of the Dharma Cloud (or *Shakti*, or *Sambhogakaya*, or Clear-Light Energy, or Holy Spirit, or Mother Light) with the "vine" of the yogi's consciousness (or *citta*, or soul, or son light) in the Heart-cave (or *Tathagatagarbha*). This union results in the severing of the Heart-knot (which Gauta-ma called the Heart-release), thereby permanently disentangling one's Self (or Buddha)-nature from the defilements of the first seven forms of un-en-Light-ened consciousness.

Who or What descends into Lanka to en-Light-en the *bodhisat-tva* (the en-Light-enment-seeking disciple)? The *Bhagavan* (Red Pine's term in his text *The Lankavatara Sutra: Translation and Com-mentary*), which D.T. Suzuki, in his translation of the *Lankavatara Sutra*, translates as the "Blessed One." The *Bhagavan*, or Blessed One, as Blessing Power (the *Sambhogakaya*, or Clear-Light Energy, or Dharma Cloud, or *Shakti*), does. On the first page of Chapter One, Red Pine writes, "The Bhagavan had been expounding the dharma for seven days in the palace of Sagara, the Serpent King." The seven days represent the seven forms of consciousness prior to the en-Light-ening eighth. Sagara is one of eight serpent kings who acted as protector of the Dharma (really, protector of the re-alization of the *Dharmakaya*). Sagara's residence was at the bottom of the ocean, which is analogous to the *Tathagatagarbha*, the ir-reducible root of Consciousness in a human. Sagara, the eighth Serpent King, represents the Heart (or Gordian)-knot, the final guardian of the Gate to the *Dharmakaya*. The Serpent King is an-other name for *Kundalini*, the "Coiled One"—and when the final, Heart "coil" is "straightened" by the Blessing Power (or Clear-Light Energy) of the Blessed One, then the *bodhisattva* morphs into a Buddha, a *Tathagata* who dwells timelessly in, and as, the *Dharmakaya*, universal Mind, or Awareness.

The Blessed One equates Mind-awakening with the tenth and final stage of Buddhahood, known as the Great *Dharmamegha*. This is likewise the final stage of Self-realization in Patanjali's yoga system; hence Buddhism coincides with classical Hindu yoga at this point.

What is the *Dharmamegha*? Although I'm no fan of the late Osho (Bhagwan Shree Rajneesh), he summarizes it nicely: "Dharmamegha means that the Self-nature has started show-ering you, and you yourself become bathed in it, drown in it."

In the *Lankavatara Sutra*, the Blessed One describes the *Bodhi-sattva's* final stage thus: "Going through the successive stages of *Bodhisattvahood*, he finally reached the state of the Dharma Cloud [*Dharmamegha*]."

To the spiritual cognoscenti, the *Dharmamegha* (or Dharma Cloud) is the culmination of *Shaktipat*, meaning the unobstructed descent of *Anugraha-Shakti*, the Holy Spirit, or *Sambhogakaya*, as the Blessing Power that transforms a *bodhisattva* into a Buddha, a Blessed One. When this Clear-Light Energy unites with contracted Mind, or *Siva* (*Alaya-vijnana*, or *citta*), in the *Tathagatagarbha* (the womb of the Buddhas, which is an analogue for the Hindu Heart-cave, or *Hridayam*), then Mind shines freely as *Bodhicitta*, or *Siva-Shakti*.

I read Red Pine's The Lankavatara Sutra, *and his explanation of mind doesn't match yours.*

Correct. And since I addressed this in detail in *Zen Mind, Thinker's Mind*, I'll simply repeat what I wrote regarding Mind versus mind.

Mind Versus mind

The real problem with contemporary scholars who write on the LS is that they have no grasp of Yogacara's Mind-Only (Cittamatra) Dharma. For example, in the first paragraph of Chapter One in his book *The Lankavatara Sutra: Translation and Commentary*, Red Pine translates a sentence in the *Sutra* as follows: "[Bodhisattvas] skilled in the knowledge that external objects are perceptions of one's own mind…" Contrast this with D. T. Suzuki's translation: "The Bodhisattva-Mahasattvas… all well understood the significance of the objective world as the manifestation of their own Mind."

Unbeknownst to Red Pine, Mind (the *Alaya*, the Unborn Substratum) is a metaphysical "Substance," and the world is the objectification or manifestation of this Mind. This point of view, called Cittamatra (or Consciousness-Only), is in diametrical opposition to Red Pine's point of view, called Vijnaptimatra (or mind-only), which sees the world as nothing but ideas, with no Reality or realities behind them, reducing all *dharmas* (or things) to mere mental projections, or representations, of one's individual mind. External objects, however, are not, as Red Pine asserts, perceptions of one's own mind. If you believe that the computer you're using now wouldn't exist just as it is after you stop perceiving it, you have evicted yourself from reality.

Red Pine doesn't understand that universal, transcendental Mind (with a big "M"), the unmanifest *Alaya*, or *Dharmakaya*, has manifested as the universe of existents, that, as Mind-"Substance," it has modified itself as stepped-down vibrations of energy and matter into the totality of phenomena. And his gross and egregious misunderstanding effectively destroys his entire analysis of the *Lankavatara Sutra*, rendering it essentially worthless. Red Pine has read Buddhist scholars such as Florin Sutton (author of *Existence and Enlightenment in the Lankavatara Sutra*) and Dan Lusthaus (see my review of his *Buddhist Phenomenology* in my Kindle *Buddhist Book Reviews for Smarties*), and these so-called "experts" on Yogacara have doubtless infected his brain with their exoteric, non-spiritual, psychologized interpretations of the Mind-Only teaching.

The viewpoint that Mind, the *Alaya*, or *Dharmakaya*, has become everything is hardly heterodox (even though modern Buddhist scholars reject it). It is the same one espoused by Zen masters Hui Neng and Huang Po, Yogacara masters Saraha and Padmasambhava, Dzogchen master Longchen Rabjam, and numerous others. Here's a quote from Saraha, from the book *Principal Yogacara Texts*:

> Thus know that the whole appearance is the Dharmakaya. All sentient beings are the Buddha. All cosmic arisings and events are from the beginning not other than the Source of Phenomena (Dharmadhatu). For this reason, everything that one can identify conceptually is as unreal as are the horns on a rabbit.

So we should regard all phenomena as unreal, and only the Source of Phenomena as real?

At your own peril. For as Ayn Rand makes clear, you can evict yourself from reality, but not from the consequences of such eviction. And as I earlier stated, while only the Source of Phenomena, viz., Mind, is Ultimately Real, all phenomena stemming from it are phenomenally real, because nothing unreal can come from the Real.

The 36 Tattvas

Divine (Unmanifest) Order (1-5)
Siva   Divine Mind (Being-Consciousness)
Shakti   Divine Spirit (Light-Energy)
Sadasiva   Divine Will
Isvara   Divine Mastermind
Sadvidya   Divine Creator

Veils of (Universal) Concealment (6-11)
Maya   Universal act of division/concealment
Kala   Reduction of power/sovereignty
Vidya   Reduction of omniscience/knowledge
Raga   Reduction of bliss/satisfaction
Kaala   Reduction of timelessness to time
Nityati   Reduction of spacelessness to space/place

Veils of the Limited Individual Subject (12-13)
Purusa   Contracted individual experient
Prakriti   Subject's experience of material reality

3 Organs of Mental Operation (14-16)
Buddhi   "Higher mind," discriminating intelligence
Ahamkara   Separate-self sense; contracted ego-"I"
Manas   "Lower mind," conceptual faculty

5 Powers of Sense-Perception (17-21)
Ghranendriya   Smelling
Rasanendriya   Tasting
Caksurindriya   Seeing
Sparsanendriya Feeling by touch
Sravanendriya   Hearing

5 Powers of Action (22-26)
Vagindriya   Speaking
Hastendriya   Handling
Padendriya   Locomotion
Payvindriya   Excretion
Upasthendriya   Sex and urination

5 Primary Elements (Tanmatras) of Sense-Perception (27-31)
Sabda   Sound
Sparsa   Touch
Rupa   Color
Rasa   Flavor
Gandha   Odor

5 Gross Elements (Mahabhutas) (32-36)
Akasha   Space
Vayu   Air
Teja/Agni   Fire
Apas   Water
Prthivi   Earth

Diagram 1. The 36 Tattvas

CHAPTER FIVE

Kashmir Shaivism: The Involution of Ultimate Reality

The tantric tradition of Kashmir Shaivism (KS), per the late eminent Hindu scholar Jaideva Singh (1893-1986), "is the culmination of Indian thought and spirituality." In contrast to Advaita Vedanta (which many, mistakenly, consider the foremost nondual yogic tradition), KS views *Maya* (phenomenal reality) as real, rather than an indeterminate illusion. Because Advaita Vedanta regards manifest existence as unreal, its "nonduality" does not qualify as true nonduality.

Since it is beyond the scope of our discussion to provide a comprehensive elaboration of KS, I suggest that those interested in the tradition refer to my Spiritual Reading List for recommended texts on the subject. That said, I hope that our consideration of the KS tradition provides a sufficient and unique explanation of its schema, both before and after the manifestation of the "rolled out" universe.

The KS schema or system consists of 36 *tattvas* (constituents or principles) which provide a map [see Diagram 1] of unmanifest Reality's descent into, and through, the manifest dimensions of *Maya*. [See *Tattvas* in the Glossary for summary definitions of the 36 *tattvas*.] Unmanifest Reality, Being-Consciousness, personified as *Siva*, the Single Existent, became/becomes all existents, while not being implicated by any of them. Because all existents stem from boundless *Siva*, appearing and disappearing in Him, the Kashmir Shaivism system is nondual, as the totality of the universe is contained within, and derives from, Him, the One Mind, or Being-Consciousness.

While *Siva's* Essence is Mind, or Consciousness, His Nature is uncreated Light-Energy, personified as *Shakti*. In KS, *Shakti* is regarded a *Siva's* inseparable Divine Consort. Thus, in KS, Ultimate, or Di-"vine," Reality consists of the "vines" of *Siva* and *Shakti*, which explains why Ultimate Reality in KS is often referred to as *Siva-Shakti* rather than *Siva*.

The KS 36-*tattva* schema begins with *Siva* (1) and *Shakti* (2). Some may argue that *Siva* and *Shakti* aren't *tattvas*, but the Source and Substratum wherefrom the succeeding *tattvas* derive. Nonetheless, they are designated as such in the KS system. *Siva* and *Shakti*, as well as the subsequent three *tattvas*—*Sadasiva* (3), *Isvara* (4), and *Sadvidya* (5)—exist outside time and space, antecedent to creation. While *Siva* and *Shakti* (as *Siva-Shakti*) are the Divine Being itself, *Sadasiva, Isvara,* and *Sadvidya* describe the Divine Being's (or Mind's) intradivine "Mental transformation," as it morphs from acausal God into creator God, ready to roll out the universe.

Sadasiva is *Siva* as Divine Will (*Iccha, or Iccha-Shakti*), the Omnipotent One. At this stage in His Divine Mind, *Siva* will-fully begins to morph into the Creator God who will "Produce" His Play, the Dance of *Siva*, a.k.a. the universe. He assumes the role of Isvara (*Jnana, or Jnana-Shakti*), the Omniscient One, and "Masterminds" His forthcoming Descent into space-time. Then, as *Sadvidya* (*Kriya, or Kriya-Shakti*), the Creator God, *Siva*, the Immeasurable One, "Acts" by "measuring out" His space-time universe (*Maya*).

Tattva (6) in *Siva's* creative Act is *Maya*. Phenomenal reality is "measured out" by spaceless-timeless *Siva*, and this universal space-time manifestation effectively draws a veil over Him, the Divine Self. The immediate products of *Maya* are the *tattvas* called the five *Kancukas* (coverings). These five *tattvas*—*Kala* (7), *Vidya* (8), *Raga* (9), *Kaala* (10), and *Nityati* (11)—reduce and limit *Siva*, the Illimitable One, in five ways: *Kala* contracts/cloaks sovereign power; *Vidya* contracts/cloaks omniscience; *Raga* contracts/cloaks bliss; *Kaala* contracts/cloaks timelessness; and *Nityati* contracts/cloaks spacelessness.

At this point, it should again be pointed out that *Siva*, of His own "Volition," for His own "Sport," contracts/cloaks Himself to create His "Play" of *Maya*. Moreover, although *Siva* seemingly limits Himself, in Reality, He remains illimitable, never implicated by His seeming Self-limitation.

Tattva (12) is *Purusa*, the individual subject, contracted into a point (*anu*) of self-awareness in the midst of Infinity. It is the Divine Person, *Siva*, cloaked as an empirical person/experient.

Tattva (13) is *Prakriti*, which in KS is the objective material (gross and subtle) manifestation experienced by an individual *Purusa*. Hence, in contrast to Samkhya philosophy, which equates *Prakriti* with the primordial elemental matrix and the manifestation of the universe referred to as "nature," KS "personalizes" "impersonal" *Prakriti*.

Next are the "*tattvas* of mental operation": *Buddhi* (14), *Ahamkara* (15), and *Manas* (16). *Buddhi*, the first *tattva* of *Prakriti*, is the intellect, the discriminating intelligence of the mind. It is sometimes referred to as the "higher mind." *Ahamkara* is the separate-self sense, or contracted I-consciousness. *Manas* is the mind that processes and mediates sensory information and habit-tendencies. It is sometimes referred to as the "lower mind."

The following "*tattvas* of sensible experience" (17-31) are products of *Ahamkara*. These are the "five powers of sense-perception" (*Jnanendriyas* or *Buddhindriyas*): smelling (*ghranendriya*), tasting (*rasanendriya*), seeing (*caksurindriya*), feeling by touch (*sparsanendriya*), hearing (*sravanendriya*); the "five powers of action" (*Karmendriyas*): speaking (*vagindriya*), handling (*hastendriya*), locomotion (*padendriya*), excreting (*payvindriya*), sexual action and restfulness (*upasthendriya*); and the "five primary elements of perception"(*Tanmatras*): sound-as-such (*sabda-tanmatra*), touch-as-such (*sparsa-tanmatra*), color-as-such (*rupa-tanmatra*), flavor-as-such (*rasa-tanmatra*), odor-as-such (*gandha-tanmatra*).

The "five gross elements" (*Mahabhutas*), the so-called "*tattvas* of materiality" (32-36), complete the KS schema. These are *akasha* (space), *vayu* (air), *teja* or *agni* (fire), *apas* (water), and *prthivi* (earth).

Those familiar with the twenty-five *tattvas* of Samkhya philosophy (which Patanjali's *Yoga Sutras* is based on) will recognize that the final twenty-five *tattvas* of the KS system are common to Samkhya (although KS interprets *tattvas* 12 [*Purusa*] and 13 [*Prakriti*] differently), and that it is the first eleven *tattvas* of the KS system that distinguish it. These eleven *tattvas* transform Samkhya from an atheistic and dualistic system into the deistic and nondualistic one of KS, which depicts how the uncreated Deity, *Siva*, the One Mind, or Being-Consciousness, as Creator God, became everything created.

Do you agree with KS's hierarchical schema of emanation / manifestation?

It's intriguing and elegant, but could be improved. First off, I would change the order of the *tattvas* by moving the *Mahabhutas* (which literally means Great, not gross or material, elements) from the bottom of the *tattva* hierarchy to the position directly after the *Kancukas*, before *Purusa* and *Prakriti*.

Here's my rationale: First, the fact that KS reduces *Prakriti* (as Samkhya defines it) from an eternal, universal Creatrix to a personal experience of objective manifestation implies that *Akasha*, the ether, the universal space element, should supersede it in the KS hierarchy. From my perspective, *Akasha* is the formless, most subtle *pranic* "substance" from whence all manifestation, including so-called "quantum" activity, arises. As such, though it is created, I view it as the elemental essence of the principle of *Prakriti* (as Samkhya construes it).

Second, without the ether and its four derivative elements (fire, earth, air, water) as a substrate, there can be no further creation, meaning no living *Purusas* to experience their *Prakriti* and embody the remainder of the *tattvas* in the KS hierarchy. *Maya tattva* contracts/cloaks spacelessness and timelessness (meaning spaceless, timeless God, or Mind, or *Siva*), which signifies that, as *Maya-Shakti*, God/Mind/*Siva* has morphed into the ether (*Akasha*), the all-pervading space element, or "substance," and that separate, created existents (or objects) moving/changing successively in that ethereal space result in, or reflect, time. Without space and time, there can be no distinct, dynamical objects; and without the four basic elements (fire, earth, air, water) that proceed from the ether, there can be no elementally constituted, physically embodied beings as living *Purusas*.

Until our present discussion, I hadn't pondered why KS and Samkhya have *Akasha* (*tattva* 32) being produced from sound, *Sabda* (*Shabda*) *tanmatra* (*tattva* 27), nor had I bothered to check if anyone else agreed with my POV regarding *Akasha's* position in the *tattva* hierarchy. Upon Googling the subject, I found an article, "Akasha (Space) and Shabda (Sound): Vedic and Acoustical Perspectives" by M.G. Prasad, Department of Mechanical Engineering, Stevens Institute of Technology,

Hoboken, New Jersey, which provides enlightening information on the "evolutionary" (really involutionary) order of
the elements:

> The evolutionary order of elements is also stated in a more
> explicit way in Bramhanandavalli of Taittriyonanishat in
> Krishna Yajurveda in the following statements [9]. Tasmat
> va etasmaat atmana akashaha sambhutaha Akashat vayuh,
> vayoragnih, agnerapaha Adbhayah prithivi, prithivya oshad-
> hayaha Oshadhibhyo annam, annat purushaha.

> The meaning of the statements is as follows: from that
> verily, from this self (Atman) is Akasha (space) born; from
> akasha, the air; from air the fire; from fire the water; from
> water the earth; from earth the plants; from plants the food;
> from food the man. It is given in the above statements that
> the production of elements begins from the all-pervading
> Atman (Brahman). Then the first element Akasa is born,
> here akasha refers to absolute space (which is mistaken for
> vacuum). This most subtle element akasha is qualified by
> sound as its property or guna.

Apart from its tattvas *order, do you have any other problems with the
KS paradigm?*

It's limited, in that it's purely spiritual, only describing Divine
descent as it pertains to *Siva* becoming man. Unlike the classical Kabbalistic Tree of Life, which is essentially hermetic, KS
cosmology doesn't venture into the occult. And unlike Hegel's
phenomenology of Spirit, which focuses on Spirit's dialectical
action in history, teleologically moving man toward God, it
neglects the evolutionary effects and impact of Spirit across
the ages. My goal in our talks, and in the resulting book it
will produce, is to innovatively combine these three different
descriptions of Divine descent into a single new paradigm.

The major problem I have with KS isn't its *tattva* order or its purely spiritual orientation; it's with those such as prominent KS scholar Christopher Wallis, who pervert Kashmir Shaivism by misrepresenting its Mind-Only doctrine as a mind-only one, while also "polluting" it with quantum crapola. In our next session [see Chapter Six], I'll present my critique of Wallis's mind-only version of KS. Then, in a forthcoming discussion, we'll again consider KS—this time in relation to the Kabbalistic Tree of Life. So, if the material I've presented on the KS schema in our current discussion seems somewhat overwhelming, it should become less so when we reconsider it.

How about KS as a philosophy of sadhana? *The 36* tattvas *describe* Siva's *descent into contraction, especially as it pertains to human souls. But they don't provide a prescription for the way out of self-contraction and into liberation* (moksha).

It is beyond the scope of our current discussion to consider the three defilements (termed the "three *malas*" in KS) that bind sentient beings to *samsara*. And the same can be said about the four means (termed the "four *upayas*") that lead beings from *samsara* to liberation. That said, the final chapter in *Nonduality and Mind-Only through the Prism of Reality* [see Chapter Sixteen] will provide detailed instructions on KS *Shaktipat* yoga/meditation, which is the same practice I call Plugged-in Presence, Power-of-Now Meditation, and Holy (or Divine) Communion.

CHAPTER SIX

The Perversion of Kashmir Shaivism's Mind-Only Doctrine

My Critique of Christopher Wallis's KS Teachings

Kashmir Shaivism (KS) is a "dead tradition," because with the death of Swami Lakshman Joo (in 1991), the last in the unbroken chain of KS lineage holders (which dated back more than a millennia), there are no longer any "official" masters in the tradition. Nonetheless, thanks to the writings of Lakshman Joo and the even better writings on the tradition by Jaideva Singh, Deba Brata SenSharma, and Paul Muller-Ortega, we now have books that provide us with enlightening translations of, and commentaries on, the major canonical texts of the tradition.

When, in bookstores in the early 1990s, I encountered the SUNY series of books on Kashmir Shaivism, edited by Professor Paul Muller-Ortega, I was blown away by the profundity and esotericism of these texts. Thanks to these texts (especially *The Philosophy of Sadhana* and *The Doctrine of Recognition*), my understanding of the En-Light-enment project expanded significantly, particularly as it pertained to *Shaktipat*, nonduality, and Mind (or Consciousness)-Only metaphysics.

A decade later, when it became clear to me that the same Kashmir Shaivism texts that had influenced my thinking had also influenced the thinking of Adi Da Samraj (as evidenced in his writings), I contacted Muller-Ortega to get his take on the Adi Da/KS tie-in. Specifically, I wanted to know if he thought that Adi Da's teachings were primarily original, or mainly derived from the KS tradition.

Through our email exchanges, I learned that Muller-Ortega was a secret fan of Adi Da's teachings, but for professional reasons, he didn't want that known. (Now, long after he has retired from girdled academia, his appreciation of Da's teachings can freely be revealed.) In 2005, I connected Muller-Ortega with a friend of mine, an influential Adi Da devotee, who was able to arrange an intimate *Darshan* with Da for him. Muller-Ortega loved it, then wrote the Foreword to Adi Da's book *The Gnosticon,* wherein he recounts his *Darshan* experience.

Interestingly enough, whereas Muller-Ortega is a huge Adi Da fan, as am I, his most prominent KS student, Christopher Wallis, who studied under him at the University of Rochester, isn't. Wallis, who obtained a PhD in Sanskrit from U.C. Berkeley, has since risen to prominence as perhaps the most popular Western teacher of tantra and KS. And while he is considered an esteemed authority on these subjects by many, I'm not one of the many.

I first encountered Wallis's teachings several years ago in his book *Tantra Illuminated*. This text informed me that Wallis had not "cracked the code" of KS, that he was merely an "uninitiated" scholar, not a sagacious yogi-pundit. Then, in 2017, Wallis published *The Recognition Sutras: Illuminating a 1000-Year-Old Spiritual Masterpiece*, which is his discourse and commentary on *Pratyabhijnahrdayam*, the canonical text of the KS Pratyabhijna (or Self-Recognition) system, as articulated by Ksemaraja in probably the tenth century.

Ksemaraja was a brilliant student of Abhinavagupta (the legendary scholar-saint credited for the comprehensive systemization of KS), and in *Pratyabhijnahrdayam* he presents the authoritative digest of the Pratyabhijna system, the highest, most esoteric teaching of Kashmir Shaivism. Long before reading Wallis's *The Recognition Sutras*, I had already deeply studied and grokked *Pratyabhijnahrdayam* through the texts *Pratyabhijnahrdayam: The Secret of Self-Recognition* by Jaideva Singh (the foremost 20th-century KS scholar) and Paul Muller-Ortega's upgraded, expertly edited version of it, *The Doctrine of Recognition*. So, having "cracked the code" of KS, I was hardly a neophyte when I applied my critical eye to Wallis's *The Recognition Sutras*. And after reading it, I wrote the following 2-star Amazon review (since deleted by Amazon, along with my 300 + other book reviews).

My Review of *The Recognition Sutras* (Christopher Wallis)

The Tantric Woo-Woo of Christopher Wallis

I've read two other versions of *Pratyabhijnahrdayam* (which Christopher Wallis has as *Pratyabhijna-hrdaya* and translates as "The Recognition Sutras"), so I was already familiar with Ksemaraja's work before reading Wallis's translation/explanation. What disturbs me somewhat is that not a single other reviewer of this book seems to have read any other version for comparison with Wallis's.

I encountered major "problems" with Wallis's exegesis and elaboration of *Pratyabhijna-hrdaya*, which I'll now explain. Firstly, I take umbrage with Wallis's "marriage" of idealist monism (which asserts that all that exists is Consciousness) and quantum physics, which he uses throughout his discourse to elaborate Ksemaraja's text. I have issues with Wallis's "marriage" because I believe that it not only misrepresents what nondual Tantric Shaivism is really about, but also provides a warped view of idealist monism and quantum physics. I have pages of notes regarding my criticisms of Wallis's "marriage," but because this is just a review and not a book, I'll limit my number of responses to Wallis's statements.

WALLIS: As quantum physicists have now thoroughly demonstrated, it is meaningless to talk of the existence of even a particle of matter without an observer; before observation, there is only probability, potentiality. Observation is creation.

MY RESPONSE: Physicists have not thoroughly demonstrated this, and many debunk it. And even if it were true on the quantum level, it is not true on the macroscopic level. Nobody can create anything in the visible world through observation.

WALLIS: There is only your consciousness manifesting the various qualia of your experience. Thus, focusing on something is actually manifesting it in more detail.

MY RESPONSE: Focusing on something does not make it manifest in more detail. You simply notice more detail because you are focusing on it.

WALLIS: Your assumption that things exist without a perceiver to perceive them is just that: an assumption. It cannot be proven.

MY RESPONSE: Not everything is being perceived at every moment, yet things continue to exist when they aren't perceived. Furthermore, cameras and scientific instruments prove this. Scientists have dated the Earth and the universe, and they existed before living beings perceived them.

WALLIS: In other words, the very fact that it [an object] is manifest within Awareness and known only through being illuminated by Awareness demonstrates that it can be nothing but Awareness.

MY RESPONSE: No, it doesn't. It only demonstrates that awareness is necessary to be aware of an object.

WALLIS: There is no reality to whatever you are aware of apart from your awareness of it.

MY RESPONSE: Yes, there is. Only someone suffering from extreme cognitive dissonance believes that there is no reality apart from their awareness of it.

WALLIS: Perception is creation, and that you—what you really are—are the creator (and sustainer and dissolver) of everything you experience.

MY RESPONSE: Your cat and dog perceive you. Did they create you? You aren't the creator of everything you experience. I've never met anyone who can create even a flea or a cockroach, let alone an elephant or a whale.

WALLIS: But the apparent common sense of that assumption has now been deconstructed by the most advanced branch of science we have, that of quantum physics. It has demonstrated that the belief in observer-independent reality is nothing other than that: a belief. And one without any evidence whatsoever to support it. Ksemaraja reveals this truth in these words: "Whatever one is aware of in this world, its nature is nothing but that awareness." Another way of saying the same thing is: there is no reality to whatever you are aware of apart from your awareness of it. "But wait a second," you say. "If I experience a specific thing, let's say a tree, and then when I'm not there my friend experiences the same thing and reports it to me, surely that proves its existence is independent of my awareness?" No—it only demonstrates that perceivers are coordinated, which we discussed back in Chapter Three. They agree on the tangible aspects of reality because their awarenesses co-create that reality, giving rise to the illusion of objectivity. But perceivers are and must be coordinated simply because they are all instantiations of a single underlying Perceiver.

MY RESPONSE: Quantum physics has not demonstrated that belief in observer-independent reality is nothing more than a belief. Nobel Prize-winning physicist Richard Feynman said, "Nature does not know what you are looking at, and she behaves the way she is going to behave whether you bother to take down the data or not." Whatever one is aware of is not that awareness, and it has reality even if one is unaware of it. The idea that perceivers co-create the same reality, giving rise to the illusion of objectivity, is absurd. Furthermore, perceivers do not always perceive the same reality.

Per Wikipedia.org under the entry Observer Effect (Physics):

"The need for the 'observer' to be conscious has been rejected by mainstream science as a misconception rooted in a poor understanding of the quantum wave function and the quantum measurement process."

What I'm going to do now is shift my focus to briefly critiquing Wallis's spiritual exegesis and elaboration of *The Recognition Sutras*. As my critique of his statements makes clear, I have little regard for Wallis's spiritual hermeneutics, which I find superficial, imprecise, and, at times, misleading. Since this is just a review, I can only, sans extensive detail, identify a few of the problems I have with his explanations. Again, I quote Wallis from his book, then provide my responses.

WALLIS: If we oversimplify a little bit, we can say that *Sakti* [*Shakti*] practices are those dynamic practices that emphasize Energy, such as yoga *asana*, energy-body practices, *pranayama*, mantra, working with thought-constructs, and so on.

MY RESPONSE: The practices Wallis describes are *sakti* (and not *Sakti*) practices because they pertain to stepped-down cosmic energies (including *prana*) and not to pure Spirit, or Clear-Light Energy, which is *Sakti*, the Force-flow of Consciousness Itself (*Siva*). In truth, the only true *Sakti* practice is that of conducting and merging with the Spirit-Power (or Current) of Consciousness. Wallis, however, fails to differentiate between *saktis* (which are created, or manifest, energies) and *Sakti* (which is uncreated, or unmanifest, Energy).

WALLIS: Now, *citta* is a word that we translate as 'mind' but is more accurately rendered 'heart-mind' in English because it is the locus of both thought and emotion, these being inextricably linked. It is therefore no surprise that Ksemaraja argues that the *citta* is the primary locus of our limited sense of self, our sense of our separate, different, and independent identity.

MY RESPONSE: *Citta* is better defined as one's individual consciousness than as one's mind because it implies the intersection of *Cit* (universal Consciousness) and *manas* (the individual mind). *Citta* is rendered heart-mind because the intersection of universal Consciousness and the "root" of the mind (in the form of *samskaras*, subconscious psychical seed tendencies), is located in the Heart-center (*Hridayam*, as distinct from the *anahata*, or heart, *chakra*).

Wallis, in his glossary, defines *Citi* as Consciousness, or Awareness, when it, more properly, should be defined as Consciousness-Power. *Cit* (which isn't even in his glossary) is the Sanskrit equivalent of Consciousness, or Awareness. Wallis knows this, and he knows that *Citi* means Consciousness-Power—but because attention to detail is lacking in this slovenly-edited text, it is tainted with errors.

WALLIS: First, he [Ksemaraja] invites you to place your mind in the Heart. In the specific language of the nondual Saiva Tantrikas, the Heart is a synonym for *bodha*, awareness. So to place the mind in the Heart, or entrust the mind to the Heart, is simply to bring reverent attention to awareness itself—to focus on the fact of being aware.

With one's sense-faculties dissolved in the space of the Heart—in the innermost recess of the Lotus—with one's attention on nothing else: O blessed Lady, one will obtain blessedness (*saubhagya*). Though any of the cakras [chakras] can be visualized as a lotus, the heart is described as such much more frequently than the others.

MY RESPONSE: What "dooms" Wallis's exegesis and elaboration of "The Recognition Sutras" to mediocrity (or less) is his failure to "crack the code" of the text. The text's title in Sanskrit is *Pratyabhijnahrdayam*, which translates into "The Heart of Recognition," but Wallis doesn't grok what the Heart (*Hridayam*) is truly about. Hence his exposition never moves beyond the surface level.

The Heart is a synonym for the Self (Divine Being-Awareness), and the Self, in an embodied human, can only be Realized (or Recognized) in, at, and through the Heart-space (or Heart-locus), which is felt-experienced two digits to the right of the center of one's chest. This is the "place" where universal Consciousness intersects (and outshines) individual consciousness. Hence, the immanent Heart (*Hridayam*) must be distinguished from the heart cakra (*anahata*)—but Wallis fails to do this.

To reduce the Heart to mere "awareness" (uncapitalized), as Wallis does, is to misrepresent the Heart. And one doesn't "place one's mind in the Heart." What occurs yogically is that the mind and sprouting *vasanas*, or habit-energies, which Wallis mistakenly equates with *samskaras* (the psychical seed tendencies that concatenate into and "sprout" as *vasanas*), are literally, via intense *Shaktipat*, sucked into the Heart-center (or *Hridayam*-locus).

Wallis is a competent writer—until it comes time to describe, in detail, the esoteric aspects of yoga and Awakening. I made this clear in my four-star Amazon review of his book *Tantra Illuminated*, and it bears emphasis here, because this liability alone undermines *The Recognition Sutras*. And when this liability is coupled with the faulty science and twisted ontological epistemology that permeate this text, what you have is a recipe for a literary failure.

If Wallis wants to up his game as a spiritual writer, he needs to move beyond Adyashanti, Nisargadatta Maharaj, and Byron Katie, all of whom he lauds in this book, and none of whom, in my opinion, were/are Enlightened (or capable of elaborating the esoteric details of Self-Awakening). He needs to read the esoteric teachings of Adi Da (available in dozens of his books) and Ramana Maharshi (available especially in *Sri Ramana Gita*, *Sat Darshana Bhashya*, and the original, un-dumbed-down *Talks with Sri Ramana Maharshi*). Da and Ramana, unlike Adyashanti, Nisargadatta, and Katie, were true Heart masters who describe, in unmatched detail, the Heart and Heart-Awakening.

Finally, Wallis needs to find himself a qualified editor, because the Kindle edition of this book could hardly have been more poorly edited. The spacing mistakes between words and paragraphs are legion, margins are mangled, and capitalization of terms is inconsistent. Most importantly, he needs an editor steeped in Tantric Shaivism to refine his prose. And the ideal choice for this would be Paul Muller-Ortega, a now-retired professor (but still active Kashmir Shaivism teacher) who taught Wallis as an undergrad. Muller-Ortega edited the (now out-of-print, but available as an ebook) *The Doctrine of Recognition* by Jaideva Singh, which provides a much deeper and richer presentation of Ksemaraja's *Pratyabhijnahrdayam* than Wallis's *The Recognition Sutras*.

Sadhguru, Another Perverter of Tantric Shaivism

Christopher Wallis is not the only perverter of Tantric Shaivism's Mind (or Consciousness)-Only teaching. Just a few days ago, at Facebook, I came across this quote from Sadhguru, probably, at this time, the most popular guru in the world: "*Shiva* is that which is, and *Shakti* is that which is not. They are two aspects of the same reality." Unbeknownst to Sadhguru, who is not a true Sat Guru, but an un-en-Light-ened pop guru pretending to be one, *Shiva* (or *Siva*) is Consciousness (or Mind) itself, and *Shakti* is *Siva's* Spirit-Power, or Light-Energy, and not "that which is not."

CHAPTER SEVEN

Kabbalah: Descent of the Divine through the Four Worlds

Kabbalah Beyond Judaism

[The following consideration of the theosophical Kabbalah is redacted from conversations with my students, and it will comprise the core of my forthcoming Kabbalah book, which I hope to publish in 2026.]

You're Jewish by birth, so Kabbalah should be right up your alley as an esoteric spiritual tradition. What can you say about it?

Plenty. In fact, my next book is going to be on Kabbalah. But because our discussion here will be limited to Kabbalah in the context of nonduality and Mind-Only, we won't be considering it in its totality. And before we get into our discussion, I must issue a disclaimer: All theosophy pertaining to the Kabbalistic Tree of Life, including my seminal new paradigm, which I'll elaborate in our discussion, is theoretical and impossible to prove. It is up to readers of our consideration to decide if they resonate with the current canonical Jewish Tree of Life (meaning the Lurianic Kabbalah) or vibe with my Kabbalistic vision. And, of course, they are free to reject both schemas.

Although I'm Jewish by birth, I was brought up non-religiously, with zero education in Judaism. So when I began to study Jewish mysticism, meaning Kabbalah, some fifteen years ago, I was starting from scratch. But as a crack mystic-philosopher, I was confident that I could "crack its code," thus enabling me to present a new and improved Tree of Life.

Because my views on Kabbalah transcend Judaism, I considered opting for the Western mystery tradition term "Qabalah," but I decided to stick with "Kabbalah" because I have little affinity for the Golden Dawn Hermetic Order, with whom the term Qabalah is strongly associated. Moreover, if a good Qabalah book by anyone, including those outside the Golden Dawn orbit, has been written, I haven't encountered it. Finally, because the Kabbalah tradition is not purely Jewish, but was significantly influenced by Gnosticism, Neoplatonism, and Sufism, my trans-traditional insights do not, in my view, violate the tradition; rather, they serve to upgrade it, just as the aforementioned "isms" did.

Many esteemed Qabalah books have been written by renowned authors such as Dion Fortune, Aleister Crowley, Israel Regardie, Franz Bardon, Lon Milo Duquette, and others, and you diss them all?

Yes, and in addition to the authors you mentioned, I've read at least a dozen others. For a time, I recommended Will Parfitt's *The Elements of the Qabalah* to students of mine because it comprehensively, though superficially, covers the "elements" (or aspects) of the Qabalah. But I finally rejected it too, because it likewise is hooey-infested and fails to satisfactorily explicate the Tree of Life.

Dion Fortune's *The Mystical Qabalah*, first published in 1935, is probably the most popular and best-selling Qabalah text. And its content has strongly influenced subsequent authors on the subject. But from my perspective, it epitomizes the crapola that infests every Qabalah book I've read. Because it exemplifies the bad in the Qabalah tradition, I'll now present my (since deleted by Amazon) review of it as an example of a failed exegesis of the Tree of Life.

[Note: If you're unfamiliar with the Qabalistic/Kabbalistic terms in the review, refer to their definitions in the Glossary or return to the review after I elaborate them in the course of the discussion. Different spellings of Kabbalistic terms abound; so, for clarity's sake, I've substituted my spellings for Fortune's terms, while including hers in parentheses. Refer to Diagram 2 of the classic Sefirotic Tree of Life for a schematic perspective of the terms.]

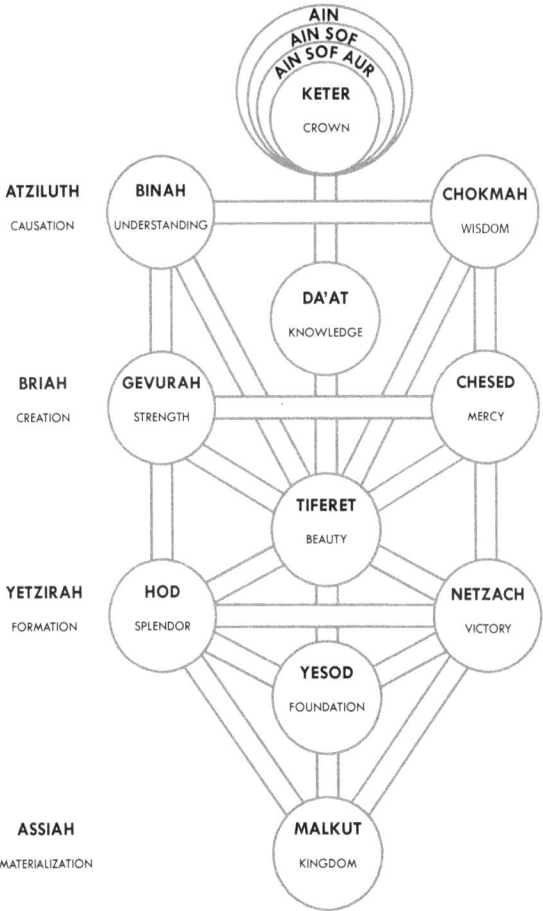

Diagram 2. The Classical Tree of Life

My Review of *The Mystical Qabalah* (Dion Fortune)

NOT the "Yoga of the West"

Dion Fortune, author of *The Mystical Qabalah*, bills her mystical Qabalah teachings as "The Yoga of the West." In her book, she makes it clear that her teachings are about the Mystical, rather than the Practical, Qabalah. She writes: "In these pages we propose to give the philosophical Tree of Life, and enough practical instruction to render it available for meditation purposes; but we do not propose to give the Practical Qabalah, which is for magical purposes; because that can only properly be learned and safely practiced in the Temple of Mysteries."

So this book, according to Fortune, is primarily about the philosophical, or cosmological-theosophical, Tree of Life and yogic, or meditation, exercises pertaining to it. Does Fortune succeed in her exegesis of the Tree of Life and the creation of a "Yoga of the West"? My answer is an emphatic NO.

First off, Fortune is almost clueless about the Tree of Life. In fact, halfway through the book, I tossed it aside because I couldn't take any more of her nonsense. I could write a book refuting her attributions and explanations, but since this is just a review, I'll limit myself to a few examples: 1) She has no understanding of *Da'at* (*Daath*), the mysterious, invisible Sefirah (Sephirah) located beneath *Keter* (*Kether*). She considers it to be "formed out of the conjunction of *Chokmah* and *Binah*." In reality, *Da'at* (*Daath*) correlates with the planet Neptune and functions as a "converter-channel" for *Keter* (*Kether*), which correlates with Pluto, transforming its Force into a flow of Divine Power, the *Ruach HaKodesh,* or Holy Spirit, which unites with *Tiferet* (*Tiphareth*), spiritually en-Lightening the Qabalist. Pluto is pressure, the atomic Force of consciousness. But for this consciousness-Force to flow, it needs an open vessel, a line of least resistance—and that is *Da'at* (*Daath*). *Da'at* (*Daath*) is invisible, open, and empty (like a vagina), allowing the phallic "thrust" of *Keter* (*Kether*) to penetrate into *Tiferet* (*Tiphareth*). 2) According to Fortune, "… if we assign to *Keter* (*Kether*) the Sphere of the Three in One, the undivided Unity, and to *Tiferet* (*Tiphareth*) the Sphere of the Redeemer or Son, we may be justified in referring to *Yesod* as the Sphere of the Holy Spirit…" Wrong again. The Holy Spirit, the "action" of the *Shekinah*, flows from *Keter* (*Kether*), Consciousness itself, and redeems the son, contracted *Tiferet* (*Tiphareth*), transforming him into the Son, or Self—En-Light-ened *Tiferet*. *Yesod* correlates with the Moon, the personal subconscious, not with the transpersonal Supernal Influx, the down-poured Holy Spirit. 3) Fortune writes: "In the Vedantan philosophy *Keter* (*Kether*) would undoubtedly equate with Parabrahma, *Chokmah* with Brahman, and *Binah* with *Mulaprakriti*." Nonsense. Parabrahma would correlate with *Ain Sof Aur* (*Ain Soph Aur*), the unspeakable Emanator of the ten Sefirot (Sephirot); *Keter* (*Kether*) with the atomic Atman, or Self (which realizes Itself in *Tiferet* [*Tiphareth*] via "marriage" with the Bride, the Holy Spirit); *Chokmah* with wisdom, the "higher mind," or ascertaining intelligence, the fourth (of five) sheaths, or *koshas*, which, per Vedanta, veil Brahman from the yogi; and *Binah* with the third sheath, which pertains to worldly understanding, the "lower mind." I could continue to deconstruct Fortune's philosophical Tree of Life, but I'll stop here out of respect for the book-review format, which is not meant for endless critiques. Instead, I'll briefly turn my attention to Fortune's "Yoga of the West."

I have devoted the past forty years of my life to studying, practicing, and teaching mystical and occult systems. I'm not only an expert in the foremost spiritual traditions—Hindu Raja Yoga,

Advaita Vedanta, and Kashmir Shaivism; Theravada, Zen, and Tibetan Buddhism; Christian Hermeticism, the mystical Kabbalah, Daism, and J. Krishnamurti's teachings—I have also practiced professional astrology and studied the I Ching and Tarot. In my opinion, Fortune doesn't know the first thing about yoga, particularly genuine Kabbalistic yoga. All she offers are rudimentary focusing exercises on abstract mental constructs pertaining to a mere map—the abstract Tree of Life. There is no such thing as a "Yoga of the West," as opposed to a "Yoga of the East." True yoga, genuine Kabbalistic yoga, knows no such distinction.

I'll now summarize real Kabbalistic yoga: Kabbalah means "to receive." And what one receives in genuine Kabbalistic yoga, which mirrors Tibetan Dzogchen and the true Christian Eucharist, is the en-Light-ening Power of Now—*Shakti*, the Holy Spirit, or *Sambhogakaya*. The union of a yogi's soul (or consciousness) with this Spirit produces Awakening, Self-realization. Kabbalah has also been described as the "work of integration," which means being integrally, or immediately and unobstructedly, present, so as to be a fit vessel for receiving and uniting with the Blessing Power from on high that transforms the Kabbalistic yogi into a Blessed One.

There is no need to even think about the Tree of Life if your only interest is the mystical Qabalah. The term "mysticism" means communion with Ultimate Reality, as Spirit. It's the exact spiritual practice that I described in the preceding paragraph. The Tree of Life is only important if you're interested in the theosophical Kabbalah—in philosophy, cosmology, and/or occult divining practices, such as astrology and the Tarot.

In sum, Dion Fortune is clueless about the Mystical Qabalah, and in my view, her book does not merit serious consideration from those looking to "crack its code."

So, are the Kabbalah books any better than the Qabalah ones?

Unfortunately, most of them also suck. In my first book, *Beyond the Power of Now*, published in 2012, I included Z'ev ben Shimon Halevi's *The Work of the Kabbalist* on my Spiritual Reading List (which I include in the back of my nonfiction books). That was a mistake, and the book is not on any of my subsequent Lists. At that time, I was still new to the study of Kabbalah and hadn't "cracked its code," but I wanted a Kabbalah book on my List, and wrongly chose Halevi's.

In the years that followed, I read numerous Kabbalah books, including ones by Michael Berg, Leo Schaya, Ann Williams-Heller, David Sheinkin, David A. Cooper, Colin A. Low, Isaiah Horowitz, Pamela Eakins, Michael Faust, Daniel Matt, Aryeh Kaplan, Gershom Scholem, and Moshe Idel; and I also read the two arguably most important Kabbalistic texts: the *Zohar* (generally considered the preeminent work on Kabbalah and Jewish mysticism) and *Sefer Yetzirah* (the earliest extant book on Jewish mysticism).

None of these books does the true "integral" (what I call "Divine") Kabbalah justice. The only one of them on my current recommended Spiritual Reading List is Moshe Idel's *Kabbalah: New Perspectives*, and that is only because it is a good academic text. Idel provides a commendable history of the Kabbalah, and he rightly understands that reception of the Supernal Influx is the essence of the mystical Kabbalah. But he has no real understanding of the theosophical (or occult) Kabbalah, and his inability to properly explicate it makes his text less than integral. Scholem's *Kabbalah* is also a worthwhile academic book for those interested in the history of the development, ideas, and leading figures of Jewish mysticism. As for a general, non-academic Kabbalah text, my choice for now is Aryeh Kaplan's *Meditation and Kabbalah*, though it too is less than stellar.

The *Zohar* does little for me, because I find it mainly a collection of pedestrian homiletic stories. As a canonical spiritual text, it's not in the same league as, say, the Hindu *Bhagavad Gita*, the Taoist *Tao Te Ching*, or the Buddhist *Lankavatara Sutra*. Moreover, it's a blatantly racist text that demonizes Gentiles. (Google "David Duke, Extermination of Gentiles" for details.) The fact that it's considered the preeminent text of Jewish mysticism bespeaks of the weakness of the Jewish esoteric tradition. *Sefer Yetzirah*, though it properly identifies the correct number of Sefirot, is full of hooey. I posted a (since deleted by Amazon) one-star review of it years ago, and here [below] is what I wrote.

My Review of *Sefer Yetzirah* (Aryeh Kaplan)

Teeming with Mystical Hokum

I first read *Sefer Yetzirah* many years ago, when I first began to study Jewish mysticism. Although I was new to Jewish mysticism, I was a long-time expert in multiple other mystical traditions, so I had a basis for comparison. In short, I was not impressed with this canonical text, which I placed in storage while I traveled the world. I recently received another copy of *Sefer Yetzirah* from a student of mine, and I reread the text, this time from the perspective of someone with substantial knowledge of Kabbalah; and again, I was less than impressed.

Before I continue with my review, I should make it clear that my negative reaction to this text is in line with my generally negative reactions to Kabbalah (and Qabalah) texts, many of which I have reviewed at Amazon. Although I think there are some good books on Jewish mysticism—I gave Moshe Idel's *Kabbalah: New Perspectives* and Aryeh Kaplan's *Jewish Meditation* four stars in my [since deleted by] Amazon reviews—I do not find Jewish mysticism a match for the foremost Hindu and Buddhist mystical texts. I am Jewish by birth, and in my view, the ancient Kabbalah is in dire need of an upgrade. Hopefully, a Jewish Avatar will emerge in the near future and "grow" a new Tree of Life.

According to Aryeh Kaplan, "*Sefer Yetzirah* is a meditative text with strong magical overtones... It appears to be an instructional manual describing certain meditative exercises." I have practiced and taught various forms of meditation—Vipassana, Zen, Dzogchen, Raja Yoga, Ramana Maharshi's Self-enquiry, Krishnamurti's choiceless awareness, et al.—and I'm not impressed with the meditative methods prescribed in this text. In my opinion, it is not a quality meditation manual.

Kaplan writes, "*Sefer Yetzirah* is one of the primary ancient astrological texts." I'm a former professional astrologer, and I find the astrology in this text to be primitive, skeletal, and based on unsound astronomical principles. Just as this is a poor meditative text, it is likewise a lousy astrological text.

Sefer Yetzirah identifies just seven "planets"—Sun, Moon, Mercury, Venus, Mars, Jupiter, and Saturn—and Kaplan opines: "Influence extends only from the visible members of our solar system. The distant planets such as Uranus, Neptune, and Pluto are not considered to have any significant astrological influence." I totally disagree with Kaplan on the influence of these planets. Furthermore, I believe that each of these planets corresponds with and, in effect, "rules" a particular Sefirah— Uranus (*Chokhmah*), Neptune (*Da'at*), and Pluto (*Keter*). In short, the Tree of Life I embrace differs markedly from the one described by *Sefer Yetzirah* and Kaplan.

Sefer Yetzirah is a short text—anywhere from 240 to 2,500 words, depending on the version—but it is replete with mystical poppycock. Because this is just a book review and not a book, I'll focus on just a few samples of its nonsense. First off, I do not believe that the universe was created from the twenty-two letters of the Hebrew alphabet, as *Sefer Yetzirah* claims. Moreover, I do not believe that these letters were "carved out of nothingness," as Kaplan puts it, because something cannot come from nothing.

According to *Sefer Yetzirah*, "He [meaning God] formed substance out of chaos, and made non-existence into existence." Existence cannot emanate from non-existence, and non-existence cannot be described as "chaotic," or as anything else. Chaos only exists from a limited human perspective. From the universal "viewpoint" of reality, chaos is impossible.

Sefer Yetzirah informs us: "The three Mothers in the universe are air, water, fire. Heaven was created from fire; earth was created from water. And air from earth decides between them... The three Mothers are the hot, the cold, and the temperate. The hot is created by fire, the cold is created from water, and the temperate from Breath decides between them." This is pure hokum: the world was not created by water, nor is cold created from water.

Sefer Yetzirah continues: "The three mothers in the Soul, male and female, are the head, belly, and chest. The head is created from fire, the belly is created from water, and the chest, from breast, decides between them." Just more hooey. Moreover, the belly, not the head, is usually associated with fire—the digestive fire and an individual's guts and vitality.

In summary, Aryeh Kaplan (1935-1983), a renowned physicist in addition to a revered Kabbalist, does a respectable job creatively elaborating upon the cryptic passages that constitute *Sefer Yetzirah*. But his creative effort fails because *Sefer Yetzirah* is too full of mystical hokum to be salvaged, and Kaplan isn't deep enough to truly grok the Kabbalah.

The Two Kabbalahs

Okay, you've dissed the classic Kabbalah and Qabalah texts. What do you offer in their stead?

Eminent Kabbalah scholar Moshe Idel, in his book *Kabbalah: New Perspectives,* argues for two distinct Kabbalahs—the "mystical-ecstatical" and the "theurgical-theosophical." I reduce the names of these two to the "mystical" (or "spiritual") and the "theosophical" (or "occult").

Kabbalah means "to receive" (or, more completely, "to face, or relate to, and receive")—and what one receives mystically and occultly, within the context of Judaism (and trans-Judaism), falls under the broad umbrella of the term "Kabbalah." Mystically, one receives what Idel calls the "Supernal Influx," which in Hebrew terms is the *Ruach HaKodesh*, the same Hypostasis, or "Body," as the Christian Holy Spirit and Hindu *Shakti*. Occultly, one receives knowledge of the Tree of Life, the emanated fundamental astral principles shaping and affecting life on earth. In other words, one receives understanding of the Hermetic principle "as above, so below."

Because the mystical Kabbalah pertains primarily to *praxis*, we'll hold off consideration of it until we turn our attention to spiritual disciplines. Our focus now will be on the occult, or theosophical, Kabbalah, given that it pertains to *theoria*, and thus the themes of nonduality and Mind-Only.

You haven't mentioned the theurgical Kabbalah, which Idel lumps with the theosophical Kabbalah.

From my perspective, Idel errs by combining the theosophical Kabbalah with theurgy (which etymologically means "divine work"). True (meaning mystical, or spiritual) theurgy pertains to invoking the Holy Spirit, not to summoning astral spirits, as Idel and most scholars and occultists have it. Hence, it should be lumped with the mystical, not the theosophical, Kabbalah.

To be fair, Idel, in one paragraph in his book, identifies drawing down the Divine Spirit as theurgic, but he fails to acknowledge that this necessarily lumps theurgy with the mystical Kabbalah.

The Theosophical (or Occult) Kabbalah

The theosophical Kabbalah is occult (or "hidden") in nature, meaning it can't be grokked by those lacking in esoteric knowledge. With this in mind, the goal in this discussion is to provide unique and arcane insights that shed light on, in order, the Three Veils of Negative Existence, the Four Worlds, *Tsimtsum* (the contraction of Consciousness-Energy), and the Tree of Life (the ten or eleven Sefirot, which are arranged into three columns, usually symbolized as pillars).

THE THREE VEILS OF NEGATIVE EXISTENCE

In conventional Kabbalistic metaphysics, three "veils of negative existence"—*Ain*, *Ain Sof*, and *Ain Sof Aur*—comprise the Matrix, or Womb, from whence the Four Worlds and the Tree of Life derive. Per conventional Kabbalah, *Ain*, the highest (or most rarified) covering, means absolute nothingness; *Ain Sof* means endlessness or limitlessness; and *Ain Sof Aur*, the lowest (or closest to the Tree of life), means endless or limitless Light.

I reject the idea of these "three veils of negative existence." I contend there is but a single "positive" veil, or Matrix, or

Womb, or Source, prior to the Four Worlds and the Tree of Life—and it is *Ain Sof Aur*, which, rightly understood, is the same Divine Being-Consciousness-Energy as Kashmir Shaivism's *Siva-Shakti*. I contend that *Ain* means no-thing, not nothing or nothingness. In other words, *Ain* signifies God not as a thing, but as the unmanifest Divine Being (or "Thing"-in-Itself) from which all manifest things derive. Although the (unmanifest) Divine Being, or Existent, is formless (empty of manifest content), it is not emptiness, because emptiness, like nothingness, is a non-existent with no ontological status. In contrast, the Divine Being (or Mind) has supreme ontological status; hence it is the Supreme Being. *Ain Sof* signifies God as limitless or infinite, meaning outside space and time. And *Ain Sof Aur* denotes God, the Divine Being (or Mind, or Consciousness), as limitless Light-Energy (or Spirit-Power); hence it is equivalent to *Siva-Shakti*—spaceless, timeless Being-Consciousness-Energy.

THE FOUR WORLDS

The Four Worlds are grossly misunderstood in conventional Kabbalah, which often, egregiously, conflates them with the four elements (fire, earth, air, and water). In fact, they have nothing to do with the four elements, but rather are the four primary dimensions of existence stemming from the Absolute, *Ain Sof Aur*. Whereas the Tree of Life pertains to our solar system, the Four Worlds are universal and describe the dimensional descent of *Ain Sof Aur* into the world of material forms.

The Four Worlds are commonly described as emanations, but from my perspective, as soon as a "world," or dimension, enters space and time, it is, by definition, created, and thus subject to destruction. Hence, strictly speaking, not all of the Four Worlds are emanations.

How about Adam Kadmon, the Original, or Primal, Man, often depict-
ed as the fifth world in Kabbalistic metaphysics?

Adam Kadmon is not an emanated or created dimension, or
"world," hence he should not be considered the fifth world.
Rather, he is the personification of the Absolute, *Ain Sof Aur*. As
such, he is an analogue for Shaivism's *Siva*, the Divine personification of Being-Consciousness, the One Mind.

The first, or highest, of the Four Worlds is *Atziluth*, considered to be "pure divinity," and as such, "near to God." It is also
referred to as the "World of Causes," meaning God's Will to
create the universe of existents, which functions under the
law of cause and effect. *Atziluth* is an analogue for Kashmir
Shaivism's *Sadasiva*, who is *Siva* as Divine Will (*Iccha,* or *Iccha-*
Shakti), the Omnipotent One. At this stage in the Divine Play,
uncreated God begins to morph into the creator God, who
will roll out the universe.

Is it proper to consider Atziluth *an emanated world or dimension?*

Atziluth is sometimes referred to as the world of emanation
itself, which implies that it isn't emanated, but rather the
Source of emanation. In reality, *Ain Sof Aur* is the Source of all
emanation, and *Atziluth*, though subsisting outside space and
time, is an emanation in the sense that it is a derivative function of the Absolute.

The second of the Four Worlds is *Briah*, the "World of Creation." It is an analogue for Plato's "World of Forms" and Kashmir Shaivism's *Isvara* (*Jnana,* or *Jnana-Shakti*), the Omniscient
One, who "Masterminds" the creative descent of *Ain Sof Aur*,
or *Siva-Shakti*, into the third world, *Yetzirah*, the ether. *Briah* is
the domain of "pure intellect," meaning God, or Mind (prior
to the emergence of space and time), "imagining," and thus

"creating," the archetypal forms that will begin to "take shape" in the ether, the primordial space element. Because its "activity" is prior to manifestation, it is an emanated dimension.

Yetzirah, the third world, is the "World of Formation," the dimension of space wherein the four basic elements (fire, earth, air, and water) that compose the physical world emerge. Unbeknownst to modern science, space is not empty but is the primal substance, or element, underlying the material world. The space element, the ether, or *Akasha*, gives rise to the four basic elements and the so-called "quantum activity" that precedes physical materialization. Many prominent occultists, most notably Franz Bardon, wrongly conflate the *Akasha* with the Absolute, when, in reality, it is a created, though subtle and invisible, dimension.

Question: Do you think that the "quantum activity" in the ether involves actual subatomic particles, as described by the Standard Model of physics, or just fluctuations or perturbations in the Akasha?

The latter, but it is beyond my understanding of physics, and outside the scope of our discussion, to consider the "etheric physics" which I believe will eventually replace both quantum physics and general relativity while providing a unified theory of physics. Those interested in the subject of etheric physics should check out Ken Wheeler's YouTube channel Theoria Apophasis and his book *Uncovering the Missing Secrets of Magnetism*. Ervin Laszlo's book *Science and the Akashic Field* is also must-reading on the subject. But I want to emphasize that although I recommend Wheeler's channel and these books, that hardly means I agree with everything they say.

The fourth "emanated" (actually created) world, *Assiah*, is the "World of Action," the material world (or universe) of differentiated existents interacting in constant flux. At this "gross" level of existence, a.k.a. *Maya*, there is maximal concealment of the Divine, as the involutionary process is complete. God's "mysterious work," through the medium of the ether, generates physical creation; and embodied, ensouled beings living in this world must undergo an evolutionary process in order to free their imprisoned souls and regain their Divine status.

TSIMTSUM, THE CONTRACTION OF CONSCIOUSNESS-ENERGY

The "Act" by which *Ain Sof Aur*, limitless Self-Conscious Light-Energy, limits Itself by contracting into the Four Worlds and the Tree of Life (or Sefirotic schema) is termed *tsimtsum* in Kabbalah. Again, this Self-limitation is only apparent because *Ain Sof Aur*, as sovereign God, or Being-Consciousness-Energy, is illimitable.

Tsimtsum, from my perspective, is the same Self-contraction and Self-limitation as *sankoca* in Kashmir Shaivism, whereby *Siva-Shakti* reduces Itself to, and "hides" Itself in, its multi-dimensional creation.

Do you think Kabbalah derived its idea of tsimtsum *from Kashmir Shaivism?*

Jewish rabbi Isaac Luria (1534-1572) revolutionized Kabbalah by introducing into it a unique concept of *tsimtsum*, and many view him as a genius for this. But my guess is that he encountered, and merely put his own "creative" spin on, Kashmir Shaivism teachings, which many centuries before had already described manifestation as the contraction and limitation of *Siva-Shakti*. According to Moshe Idel in his book *Kabbalah: New Perspectives*: "One cannot underrate the possibility that Hindu traditions infiltrated into Kabbalah, perhaps via the intermediary of Sufi material."

A comprehensive consideration of Luria's intricate theory of *tsimtsum* is beyond the scope of our current discussion, because I don't buy his paradigm nor want to spend undue time dissecting it. Those interested in delving into the voluminous and convoluted details of his *tsimtsum* can consult books on the subject. Basically, Luria theorized that God, *Ain Sof Aur*, brought empty space into being, then created vessels, the Sefirot, into which He poured His Light-Energy, the *Aur*. The originally perfectly balanced Sefirot could not contain the Light-Energy and shattered. Sparks of God's Light were carried downward with the shards of the shattered vessels, resulting in "chaos" (*tohu*), discordant separation in His universal creation. The goal of the Kabbalist, from the Lurianic perspective, is to rectify this separative disorder through a complex process whereby the Sefirot are reconfigured into *partzufim*, structured, interrelated components (in the form of Archetype Personas) which, putatively, restore universal harmony.

What are your problems with Luria's tsimtsum?

First off, the idea that God created perfectly balanced Sefirot, which then shattered from the intensity of His Light-Energy because they couldn't contain it, bespeaks of God as a Dufus, an inept creator. Who, in their right mind, would want to worship such a God? Moreover, rather than rectify His own cataclysmic screw-up, He placed the burden of repair, of establishing universal harmony (*tikkun*), upon exiled mankind, in a state of deluded separation only because of His fuckuppery.

Second, I have zero affinity for Luria's reconfigurations of the Sefirot into *partzufim*. The idea that the Sefirot, in their rectified state as *partzufim*, are then able to hold and conduct God's Light (and thus establish *tikkun*) is absurd. I don't have a clue why any clear-thinking mystic-philosopher would resonate with such an idea, whether it's viewed literally or figuratively. What's even more absurd is the idea that humans, specifically "God's chosen people," the Jews, can somehow, through their religious efforts, engender such universal redemption and harmony.

From my perspective, God, or Mind, purposely created our planetary solar system, with planetary spheres (Sefirot) serving as conduits (or, at least, correlates) of distinct, specific stepped-down energies, both "good" and "bad." Without the admixture of "positive" and "negative" dimensional energies, God's "play," or "dance," on Earth would be dull, lacking excitement, challenge, and drama.

What do you mean when you say the planets may serve as correlates rather than conduits?

Correlation is not causality. Just as a watch or a clock is not a conduit of time, but merely a means for correlating it with the Earth's rotation relative to the Sun, the planets may likewise provide just the means for reading astral energies/influences rather than the function of actually conveying them.

Do you have any more problems with the Lurianic Kabbalah? And what can you say about the Cordoverean Kabbalah, which was the canonical Kabbalah prior to the Lurianic?

I could go on and on, deconstructing not only Luria's Kabbalah but others' Kabbalahs as well. And I would gladly do so, in a massive tome, if someone grants me, say, 500 K for my work. I have identified my fundamental problem with Luria's Kabbalah—his ideas on *shevirath ha kelim* (the shattering of the vessels), *partzufim* (the reconfiguration of the vessels), and *tikkun* (the restoration of universal harmony)—but beyond this basic critique, it would take a major work to thoroughly deconstruct these ideas, as well as others in his teachings.

Luria wrote nothing on Kabbalah. His oral teachings were transcribed by his closest disciple, Chaim Vital. But some of Luria's other students provided differing versions of his teachings, thereby muddying what he really taught. In the end, however, Vital's interpretation of Luria's talks became canon. Regrettably, no new Kabbalah has emerged to significantly challenge the Lurianic, which, as I have made clear, is, at best, flawed, and, at worst, nonsensical.

If the Lurianic Kabbalah is as problematic as you make it out to be, why hasn't a new Kabbalah emerged to challenge its dominance?

In part 13 of his excellent 14-part series on Kabbalah and Jewish mysticism, Professor Justin Sledge, at his YouTube channel Esoterica (which I highly recommend), explains why there has been no significant further development in Kabbalah beyond the Lurianic system. According to him, it's because the Kabbalah establishment was so shell-shocked by the intratradition cataclysm resulting from the anointment of the false messiah Sabbatai Zevi by the Sabbatean movement in the mid-seventeenth century that it became gun-shy regarding any further major developments, and reactively settled on the Chaim Vital version of Luria's teaching as canon.

Interestingly enough, Professor Sledge, who bemoans the lack of Kabbalah development beyond the Lurianic system, is an outlier who prefers the preceding Cordoverean Kabbalah to the Lurianic. But I have as little regard for Cordovero's Kabbalah as I do for Luria's. I read the free online version of Moses Cordovero's *Introduction to Kabbalah* that Sledge recommends; and in addition to the text's poor writing, I was unimpressed with Cordovero's Tree of Life attributions, which are on the same pathetic level as Dion Fortune's in her text *The Mystical Kabbalah*.

When we next turn our attention to the Tree of Life, you'll see what my fundamental Sefirotic attributions are, and you can compare them to those of other theosophical Kabbalists and Qabalists, none of whom impress me. Before we begin our consideration of the Tree of Life, are there any more questions about *tsimtsum* or creation?

How about the Kabbalistic teaching that the universe was created from the 22 letters of the Hebrew alphabet?

The idea that letters (even if they have their own meaning and numerical values) are the direct (or even derivative) building blocks of creation is patently absurd. The universe was not created *ex nihilo* (from nothingness), and it was not created from letters. It was created from uncreated Mind-Energy. Letters, as well as numbers, are created symbols, not the uncreated Source (or Agency of that Source) from whence existence springs.

So you reject Hebrew gematria?

When you realize that there are many different, conflicting methods to calculate the numerical values of Hebrew words (which gematria purports to do) and that gematria probably originated in Greece from the Greek alphabet, and therefore isn't even a Jewish creation, it's hard to give much, if any, significance to its value in the study of Kabbalah. In fact, the Cordoverean Kabbalah, the standard Kabbalah prior to the Lurianic, doesn't even mention Gematria. But if occult numerology floats your boat, feel free to have fun with it.

Physicists tell us that the contracted universe is expanding (or inflating) at a speed faster than light. What is it expanding into?

For a scientific explanation, check out renowned physicist Sabine Hossenfelder's YouTube video "What Does the Universe Expand

Into." My explanation differs from Sabine's. I contend that the universe expands (or inflates) into illimitable, spaceless Mind.

THE TREE OF LIFE, PART 1

Per Wikipedia: "Jewish mysticism depicts the Tree of Life in the form of ten interconnected nodes, as the central symbol of the Kabbalah. It comprises the ten Sefirot powers in the divine realm."

The so-called "nodes," the ten Sefirot (Spheres), have been described as potencies, vessels, channels, intermediaries, instruments, hypostases, logoi, and more—but perhaps the most graphic description of them is as prisms. I say this because, as the cognoscenti know, the Sefirot are analogues for the planets (or planetary spheres) in our solar system (which, astrologically, include the Sun and the Moon), which function prismatically to channel a spectrum of energies particular to their own (Divinely designated) domains and agencies. Regarding the prismatic function of the planets, Vamadeva Shastri, in his book *Jyotisha*, *Hindu Astrology*, writes:

> In the Hindu view, the planets are not mere celestial bodies circling the Sun. They are also divine beings—shown here as they were positioned on the first morning of the current millennium. Each is like a prism, conveying subtle energy from the far galaxies, thus impacting man's affairs on Earth according to its unique nature and location in the sky.

Although, as a proponent of tropical (Sun-based) astrology, I'm not a fan of Vedic sidereal (star-based) astrology, and I reject the idea that the planets are "conveying subtle energy from faraway galaxies," I resonate with Shastri's description of the planets as prisms. And, as I will argue, it is only by correlating the prismatically functioning planets with the Sefirot that the "code" of the Tree of Life can be cracked.

When the Kabbalistic Tree of Life was first revealed (in Sefer Yet-zirah), *only seven planets—Sun, Moon, Mercury, Venus, Mars, Jupi-ter, and Saturn—had been identified; yet* Sefer Yetzirah *insists that there are ten Sefirot.*

The early Kabbalists, in accordance with the ancients before them, identified ten distinct Divine agencies, but because Uranus, Neptune, and Pluto, the three "outer" planets, had yet to be dis-covered, they couldn't correlate these agencies with the planets. With the discoveries of these outer planets, culminating with Pluto in 1930, the proper correlations became possible. When the Earth is included, the addition of Uranus, Neptune and Pluto results in eleven Sefirot; but the cognoscenti recognize that *Keter* (which corresponds with Pluto) and *Da'at* (which corresponds with Neptune) are two aspects of the same (dyadic) principle, thereby conserving the ten-order schema.

The "fathers" (meaning Cordovero and Luria) of the modern, in-vogue Kabbalah were not only ignorant of the existence of the outer planets, they also, in accordance with the Torah, con-sidered the Earth to be the center of the universe. Consequently, because of their ignorance, they did not acknowledge the solar system and differentiate it from the universe. Given their as-tronomical ignorance, how could they have possibly been able to "craft" an integral Kabbalah?

As you can see from the classic Sefirotic Tree of Life illustration [Diagram 2], simple one-word descriptions are now common-ly associated with each Sefirah. These descriptions are farcical, reductive jokes that in no way tell us what each of the Sefirah is really about. In order to understand this, one needs to study astrology. Because the Kabbalistic Tree of Life is essentially a quasi-map of the planetary solar system as a ten-dimension-al channel of astral energies, its "code" can't be cracked sans

KABBALAH: DESCENT OF THE DIVINE THROUGH THE FOUR WORLDS   65

astrology, which provides the means for a deep dive into the dominion of each planet.

Okay, you're now dissing the common one-word descriptions of the Sefirot and insisting that the complex, multi-level descriptions of the planets provided by astrology are the answer to "cracking the code" of the Tree of Life. But isn't that the same thing Luria does by re-configuring the one-dimensional Sefirot into the multi-dimensional partzufim?

There is a big difference between the astrological descriptions of the planets, which are analogues for the Sefirot, and the *partzufim*, which are an imaginary creation of Isaac Luria's mind. Innumerable people across the ages, independent of each other, have identified the same astro-attributes of the planets. In contrast to this universal recognition of planetary astro-traits, only one man, in one tradition, Luria, identified and described the *partzufim;* yet, remarkably, his vision of the Sefirot became canon, blindly accepted by the bulk of the (clearly clueless) Kabbalists who followed after him.

I'm now going to quote from Aryeh Kaplan's book *Meditation and Kabbalah* to further elucidate the *partzufim.* Then tell me if you think they are an ontic reality or a chimeric creation from a fogged-out mind:

> After having been shattered, the Vessels [the Sefirot] were then rectified and rebuilt into the Partzufim. Each of these Partzufim consists of 613 parts, paralleling the 613 parts of the body, as well as the 613 commandments of the Torah. These Partzufim were then able to interact with each other. More important, they then resembled both man and the Torah. They were therefore able to interact with man through the Torah, and they therefore became givers as well as receivers.

In their rectified state, as Partzufim, the Vessels are then adequate to receive God's Light. In the Ari's [Luria's] terminology, this state is called the Universe of rectification (*Tikkun*).

Clearly a chimeric creation from a fogged-out mind.

Exactly. No anatomy book identifies 613 parts to the body. Moreover, the idea that the *partzufim* consist of 613 parts to match the Torah limits Kabbalah to a sectarian Jewish doctrine that, in effect, "privatizes" cosmogenesis, reducing it to an exclusively Jewish reality.

The Lurianic Kabbalah's mythos is ethnocentric to the max, identifying the Jews as God's "chosen people," elected by God with the divine mission of transforming the universal chaos (*tohu*) caused by "the shattering of the vessels" (*shevirath ha kelim*) into universal cosmos (*tikkun*).

I say that an ecumenical theosophical Kabbalah, rather than Luria's parochial chimerical Kabbalah, is what's needed to properly explain the Divine's descent through the Four Worlds and its relationship with man. That said, we'll now begin our discussion of said Kabbalah and end our consideration of Luria's.

THE TREE OF LIFE, PART 2

Now that I'm done dissing Luria's *partzufim* poppycock, I'll critique the simple one-word designations commonly associated with each Sefirah and provide more detailed descriptions of them.

According to conventional Kabbalah, the ten Sefirot shine in each of the Four Worlds. While this may be true, I contend that the Sefirotic Tree of Life applies only to our solar system. Moreover, I maintain that the traditional keyword descriptions for each Sefirah—(*Keter*/Crown, *Da'at*/Knowledge, *Chokmah*/Wisdom,

Binah/Understanding, *Chesed*/Mercy, *Gevurah*/Strength, *Tiferet*/ Beauty, *Hod*/Glory, *Netzah*/Victory, *Yesod*/Foundation, *Malkhut*/ Kingship)—are grossly reductive and, in some cases, not representative of what a particular Sefirah is truly about.

The ten Sefirot no doubt existed in God's Mind prior to the creation of the solar system. Real, or hypercosmic, God is unmanifest Consciousness-Energy, and each Sefirah represents a particular dimension/expression of stepped-down Consciousness-Energy. In my view, God deemed these dimensions/ expressions the archetypal "forms" of existence and created a "mini-God," a planet, to "rule" over each of them. When God-given life on Earth evolved to the degree of manifesting conscious spiritual humans, some of these beings discovered the Sefirot, which were then correlated with the planets in our solar system.

Because each Sefirah correlates with a planet, the discovery of the outer, "transpersonal" planets—Uranus (1781), Neptune (1846), and Pluto (1930)—enabled theosophists to properly apply the art/science of astrology to Kabbalah.

Because it's fun to combine Tarot and astrology, I'll also include my Major Arcana/Sefirot correlations along with my planetary ones. Again, because I have no allegiance to any current or historical Kabbalistic Tree of Life, I have no problem "disrespecting" them by associating Tarot cards (from the uber-popular Rider-Waite deck) with the Sefirot. In fact, these correlations serve to shed additional revelatory light on the vibrational functions and energies of the Sefirot.

The highest, or most holy, Sefirah on the Tree of Life is *Keter*, which is commonly described as "Crown." *Keter* is often considered to be "above consciousness." To my mind, *Keter* is not above consciousness; rather, it represents Consciousness itself, the "atomic" human Soul, the *Atman*. *Keter* is an ideal match for Pluto, the "atomic" planet, which, in its highest expression, represents penetrating consciousness-force, or soul-power. The sage who cuts through spiritual materialism (all the "idols" of the mind) and unites his soul (or consciousness) with the Holy Spirit exemplifies pure Plutonic power.

Although *Keter* is placed at the crown of the Tree of Life, signifying its apex position in the Sefirotic hierarchy, in reality, it is ultimately the Heart of the Tree, shining as diamond-like Consciousness itself through the medium of *Tiferet*.

The Magician is the Tarot card that best correlates with *Keter*/Pluto. I see the Magician as Lord *Siva* doing his "Dance." The worlds (and everything in them) are built on Consciousness, reflecting *Keter* "magically" intersecting creation. An En-Lightened mystic who has severed the Heart-knot (and is one with *Siva*) is a master-magician, a *Siddha* with *siddhis* who can, via his Plutonic consciousness-power, "initiate" (or Spirit-baptize) others into *Siva*-Consciousness.

I contend that the Tree of Life can't be grokked without including the so-called "eleventh Sefirah," *Da'at*. And, as I will argue, this Sefirah is not really an eleventh Sefirah. Rather, it is the inseparable *Shakti* to Keter's *Siva*. In other words, *Keter-Da'at*, like *Siva-Shakti*, is a nondual dyad. Hence, *Keter-Da'at* is ultimately a single Sefirah.

Da'at is sometimes referred to as the "invisible Sefirah." This is the case because until the mystic, or Kabbalist, is "initiated" (Spirit-baptized) and receives *Siva* as *Shakti* (the Holy Spirit), he cannot "see," or perceive, this Sefirah, which is like an ineffable empty cup that becomes noticeable only after it is filled with Elixir, or *Soma*, from *Siva*/*Keter*. Once the empty cup, or Holy Chalice, is filled, *Da'at* (or "She") is revealed as the inseparable Divine Consort of *Keter/Siva* (or "He"). The popular occult image of Jesus seated in the Holy Chalice (or Grail) reflects the "birth" of the Christ/Son resulting from this Divine Union/Holy Marriage.

Just as Pluto is an ideal match for *Keter*, Neptune is the same for *Da'at*. And interestingly enough, Pluto's and Neptune's orbits cross, reflecting their biunial relationship. The highest expression of Neptune is perfect receptivity of, or openness to, the "Ray," or "Phallus," of Pluto/*Siva*/*Keter*. When Neptune (or Neptunian energy), like a vagina, receives Pluto (or Plutonian energy), then Divine Elixir, or *Soma*, is produced; and this ambrosial Light-Energy en-Light-ens the receptive (or self-nullified) mystic/Kabbalist.

The Tarot card that best correlates with *Da'at*/Neptune is the High Priestess. In fact, if you check her card, you will see that she wears the glyph for Pluto atop her head. Moreover, everything in her image bespeaks of utter receptivity to downpoured Divine Power, *Shaktipat*.

So, *Da'at* isn't "Knowledge." When reduced to a single word, She is "Reception."

You haven't mentioned the 22 paths in the Tree of Life, symbolized by the lines connecting the Sefirot. What can you say about them?

There aren't 22 paths, nor are there 32 (if the Sefirot are included). The fact that the Sefirot are interconnected does not signify paths, but rather relationships between their functions and energies. In individual astrology charts, the angular relationships between the planets (analogues for the Sefirot) are called "aspects." But aspects aren't paths; they simply describe facets of interplanetary relationships. In the Tree of Life, there are no aspects between the Sefirot: the connecting lines between them simply identify them as forming an integral schema or whole.

Returning to our Sefirotic consideration, the third Sefirah for us to consider is *Chokmah*. *Chokmah*, to my mind, is a perfect match for the planet Uranus. Uranus, like *Chokmah*, represents the "higher mind," or "Wisdom," which is the keyword commonly associated with *Chokmah*. Uranus, which is often viewed as a higher octave of Mercury, also correlates with *buddhi* (discriminating intelligence in Yoga philosophy); and as such, it is about detaching from the binding mind-forms of discursive thinking. The Tower card is an ideal match for *Chokmah*. Although it's quite common to associate this card with Mars, Uranus is a better match, and I believe that the originators of the Tarot, with this card, presciently anticipated the much later discovery of Uranus. The image of the man being unceremoniously tossed from the top of the tower conveys a powerful message: if you build a Tower of Babel (or mental babble), then attempt to spiritually awaken, be prepared to jettison all your mental baggage.

Binah, opposite *Chokmah* on the Tree of Life, clearly correlates with Saturn; and most Qabalists concur with this. The common keyword for *Binah* is "Understanding"—meaning mundane, or worldly, understanding, as opposed to the "other-worldly," or spiritual, Understanding/Wisdom of *Chokmah*. Saturn's rings represent worldly bondage to *samsara*, the circumscribed karmic circle of life—meaning contracted, sorrowful (or saturnine) becoming, as opposed to free, blissful Be-ing. The World Tarot card is the best match for *Binah*. The Devil (or Satan) card could also be considered an appropriate match, since it emphasizes the suffering inherent in dualistic worldly bondage. But I think the prominent goat horns atop the devil in the Devil card indicate that the card is meant to be a match for Capricorn, the sign of the goat.

Chesed correlates with Jupiter. The common keywords for *Chesed*—kindness and mercy—reflect Jupiter's benevolent and generous energy. No Major Arcana card is a clear-cut match for these keywords, which reflect only one aspect of *Chesed*/Jupiter. In astrology, Jupiter rules gambling and speculation; thus *Chesed* also pertains to these themes. But this is ignored in orthodox Kabbalah, which derives from moralistic Judaism, which wouldn't associate a Sefirah with gambling and financial speculation. Given the speculative nature of *Chesed*/Jupiter, the Wheel of Fortune card, rather than the Hierophant card, is the most suitable match for *Chesed*. Unlike the orthodox Kabbalists, the Tarot originators understood and took into account that life and fortune are a matter of chance.

Gevurah and Mars mirror each other. The terms "might" and "severity" aptly describe both *Gevurah* and Mars. The ram-adorned throne in the Emperor card indicates that the card correlates with either Aries or Mars, the ruler of Aries. My choice is the latter. First, it makes sense that the Emperor card, the male/yang archetype, would correlate with Mars because the complementary Empress card, the female/yin archetype, prominently displays the glyph of Venus. Second, Aries, in my view, is a match for the Fool card, since Aries leaps before it looks, and the Fool is pictured on the edge of a cliff, oblivious to his next step. Moreover, in the Rider-Waite deck, the Sun shines prominently at the top of the card, reflecting the fact that the Sun, per astrology, is exalted in Aries. It could be argued that the Strength card is a match for *Gevurah*/Mars since "Strength," the common keyword for this Sefirah, correlates with "might" and "severity." But the Lion image is a giveaway that the match for this card is the sign of Leo.

Netzach/Venus is the feminine counterpart to *Gevurah*/Mars. The keywords for *Netzach*—"Victory" and "Eternity"—are reflected by the circle above the cross in the glyph for Venus, which is displayed in the Empress card, which, as I just pointed out, clearly correlates with *Netzach*/Venus. Venus is the goddess of fertility and material growth; hence she refers to "victory" or "success" on the earthly plane. Because the "fertile" life-energy "channeled" through Venus, the nature goddess, is timeless, Venus pertains to eternal fecundity.

The most common keyword associated with *Tiferet* is "Beauty." Other keywords for this Sefirah include "Spirituality" and "Integration." I think "Integration" is the preferable keyword, because this Sefirah is essentially about self-integration/self-actualization, which, on the highest level, signifies spiritual Self/Soul/Son-realization.

It couldn't be clearer that the Sun is the planet that correlates with *Tiferet*. The Sun is the integrating planet in astrology, the central body around which the other planets revolve. The Sun Tarot card is the obvious match for *Tiferet*. The card's image—two young, naked (meaning Virgin, or unborn) lovers holding hands under the shining Sun—implicitly refers to the union of *Keter* (Pluto/Magician/*Siva*) and *Da'at* (Neptune/High Priestess/*Shakti*) in the spiritual Heart-center (or Sun), the abode of the awakened Self, or Soul, or Son.

Just as the Sun clearly correlates with *Tiferet*, the Moon is the obvious match for *Yesod*. The common keyword for *Yesod* is "Foundation," but perhaps it should be "Reflection." *Yesod*/Moon is, ultimately, the Feeling of Being, the reflective component of the Being-ness of the Self, or Son. The Moon card image depicts two dogs barking at the Moon. The Moon is unaffected by the barking (meaning emotional reactivity), and despite its apparent "crabby" phases (signified by the crab pictured underneath the dogs), it continues as the constant reflective medium (or mirror) for the Sun.

The Sefirah *Hod* is the standard match for the planet Mercury. But the usual keywords for *Hod*— "Splendor" and "Glory"— don't readily accord with Mercury, the planet that rules mentation and communication. However, if we expand our understanding of Mercury to include orienting the mind to receiving the Divine, we can understand why the Jewish Kabbalists associate *Hod* with prayer, the repetition of Divine names in order to evoke the descent of the Divine Splendor. As Wikipedia puts it, "*Hod* is where form is given by language in its widest sense, being the key to 'the mystery of form.'"

The Judgment card, in my opinion, is the best match for *Hod*/ Mercury. This card conveys two essential messages: One, "Judge ye not so ye be not judged" (meaning transcend the conventional mind, which focuses on judging); and two, answer the clarion call of the Divine (represented by the Archangel Gabriel's trumpet) in order to receive redemption in the form of Splendor and Glory from above.

The final, or bottom, Sefirah is *Malkhut*, which means "Kingdom." The Kingdom referred to here is planet Earth, divinized and glorified by the *Shekinah*, the Divine Presence and Splendor. There are no planets in astrology other than Earth that correlate with *Malkhut,* and I don't associate a Major Arcana card with it.

A few questions: First, why don't you associate a Tarot card with Malkhut? *Second, what about the remainder of the Major Arcana? Third, is it just a coincidence that there are 22 Kabbalah paths and also 22 Major Arcana cards?*

I don't associate *Malkhut* with a zodiac planet or a Major Arcana card because the zodiac planets and the 22 cards are "objects" in relation to *Malkhut*, an analogue for the Earth (and Earthlings), the "subject" and center they "revolve" around or pertain to. In the case of the remaining Major Arcana, I associate each of the cards with one of the twelve zodiac signs, but an elaboration of this association is outside the scope of our current discussion. Regarding the 22 Major Arcana cards, my guess is that they were designed to correspond with the ten Sefirot (in relation to Earth/Malkhut) and twelve astrological signs, and also, perhaps, the 22 lines connecting the Sefirot. But from my perspective, neither the planets, signs, lines, nor Major Arcana equate to "paths."

You've pretty much covered the constituents of the Tree of Life. All that seems left to consider are the Three Pillars.

All the Spheres belong to one of the Three Pillars. The left-side pillar, from top to bottom, consists of *Binah* (Saturn), *Gevurah* (Mars), and *Hod* (Mercury). It is called the Pillar of Severity because Saturn and Mars are classified as "malefics" in astrology, while Mercury is considered neutral. Saturn is cold and demanding; Mars is harsh and confrontational; and Mercury is mental, meaning unfeeling. Hence, this pillar is about the cold, hard facts and challenging nature of life.

The right-side pillar, from top to bottom, consists of *Chokhmah* (Uranus), *Chesed* (Jupiter), and *Netzach* (Venus). It is called the Pillar of Mercy because Jupiter and Venus are classified as "benefics" in astrology, while Uranus is considered neutral. Jupiter, the "Great Benefic," bestows forgiveness and blessings; Venus, the "Lesser Benefic," provides harmony and good will; and Uranus, in its highest expression, imparts wisdom, which accords with mercy.

The central pillar, from top to bottom, consists of *Keter* (Pluto), *Da'at* (Neptune), *Tiferet* (Sun), *Yesod* (Moon), and *Malkhut* (Earth). It is called the Pillar of Balance because it supposedly reconciles and integrates the opposite "poles" of the left-side and the right-side pillars. In reality, it pertains primarily to en-Light-enment, the central purpose of life. Pluto/*Keter* is transpersonal Con-sciousness-Force; Neptune/*Da'at* is reception of the flow of that Consciousness-Force as Spirit; and the Sun/*Tiferet* is personal in-tegration with the Spirit, which enables the soul of the individual mystic/yogi to shine as immanent, radiant Consciousness-Force. The Moon/*Yesod* represents subconscious emotions and feelings. When en-Light-ened by the flow of Spirit, Light-Energy from above, Moon/*Yesod* transmutes into the Feeling of Being, which is Beatitude or Bliss. Earth/*Malkhut* is the Kingdom of Heaven on Earth. When mankind, the God-appointed stewards of our planet, freely, en masse, channel Divine Light-Energy, then Heaven and Earth will be united. But don't hold your breath waiting for this to happen.

It seems that ordinary, un-baptized-in-the-Spirit individuals will not experience the central pillar, or channel, as you describe it.

Correct. It's an analogue for the central channel, the *Sushumna*, in Hindu yoga. And in most people, this channel is dormant, not yet activated by *Shakti*.

So, how will ordinary people experience the Sefirot/planets that com-prise the central channel?

Outside the context of central-channel "initiation" and partic-ipation, individuals will, consciously or unconsciously, exper-ience the central-pillar Sefirot/planets as they are described by astrology. Therefore, their experiences will be shaped and colored by the zodiacal placement of the planets, as reflected in their individual birth charts.

Summary of the Tree of Life

You've covered a lot of ground in your description of a new theosophical Kabbalah. Can you summarize what you've said and integrate it with the themes of nonduality and Mind-Only?

The Tree of Life is an intermundia between Heaven (the Divine Domain, or Mind) and Earth (the terrestrial plane). Although it exists in the context of the Four Worlds, through its agencies, the Sefirotic spheres (which are analogues for the planets), it pertains to our solar system, not the universe. The only way to deeply grok the Tree of Life, which, through its Sefirot/planets, functions like a ten-dimensional prism (refracting the universal Light-Energy of Mind into ten distinct astro-domains), is through astrology.

Rather than being the result of *tsimtsum* gone awry, as the Lurianic Kabbalah has it, I imagine the creation of our solar system as the product of Intelligent Design by the Divine Creator/Mind. And I believe that the Creator provided the planets to serve as maps and guideposts for discerning souls seeking cosmic direction.

It is beyond the scope of our current discussion to sufficiently consider astrology as it pertains to Kabbalah, but in my forthcoming Kabbalah book (due for publication in late 2026), I will attempt to do so by expanding upon the material in this discussion, while also including new information.

Regarding nonduality and Mind-Only, *Ain Sof Aur*, as Divine Mind-Energy, has become everything while not becoming anything. Its uncreated, unmanifest Clear-Light Energy, *Aur*, at the behest of Mind, morphed into a spectrum of stepped-down energies and vibrations, which crystallized into matter. And life, including ensouled life, was "programmed" by Mind to emerge from, and in, its "intelligently designed" energy/ matter matrix on planet Earth. Mind (or Consciousness) and its Energy (or Spirit) remained, and remain, omnipresent in the created world of life, energy, and matter; but as the unmanifest Substratum, they are not of the world. From a top-down, nondualistic perspective, Mind has become everything; so there is only Mind. But from a dualistic perspective, nothing created is Mind, because, unlike Mind, which is timeless and permanent, creation is time-bound and impermanent. In other words, creation takes place in Mind, and its energies and matter derive from Mind (or Mind-Energy); but that does not make it Mind.

The theosophical Kabbalah, via the Tree of Life, is a speculative schematic attempt to explain the relationship (including the cosmological history) between Heaven and Earth, Creator and created. It interposes an *axis mundi*, in the form of the Sefirot (which I equate with the planets), to "bridge the gap" between God and man.

In our next discussion, we will consider another *axis mundi* of sorts, the "World Spirit," as conceived by Hegel. In other words, we'll consider the phenomenology of Spirit (or Mind) viewed through a Hegelian lens.

CHAPTER EIGHT

Beyond *The Phenomenology of Spirit,* Part 1

Hegelian Idealism and Dialectic

You've now considered nonduality and Mind-Only in the contexts of Yogacara (Lankavatara Sutra), Zen (Huang Po), Kashmir Shaivism, and Kabbalah. What's left for you to complete your considerations?

As I stated at the end of our Kabbalah discussion, Hegel is next on our agenda. After Hegel, I'll then seek to tie together the different schools of thought that we've considered. The end product may be less than satisfactory, but it will be fun to see what happens when we attempt to integrate these various perspectives. Independent of this synthesis attempt, I'll then critique some of the prominent current voices on nonduality and Mind-Only.

Hegel, considered by many to be the most important philosopher since Kant, was a theologian devoted to philosophy as a means to disseminate gospel on God's work in the world. In a lecture, he preached: "Philosophy has no object but God and so is essentially rational theology and, as the servant of truth, a continual divine service."

Hegel, who was steeped in Eastern philosophy, espoused a view very much in accord with Kashmir Shaivism: that God became man so that man could realize God. Hegel called this realization Absolute Knowledge, and his magnum opus *The Phenomenology of Spirit* is an extensive discourse on man's progress through stages, in a social and historical context, toward this Absolute Knowledge.

For Hegel, God is Spirit or Mind (*Geist*), which is equivalent to Kashmir Shaivism's *Siva-Shakti* (Consciousness-Energy). And *Geist*, or Spirit, in the form of the "World Spirit," is embedded in man, teleologically instigating his evolution from the "fall" to "God-Union." The "World Spirit," as Hegel conceives it, is the "programmed" unfolding of Spirit in time, through man. It is God surreptitiously influencing man's consciousness, driving his evolutionary ascent, through the ages, to Absolute Knowledge.

Hegel's optimistic view of mankind as ever-evolving is contrary to Schopenhauer's, which rejects the idea that humanity is on a God-ordained ascent to Divinity.

Very true. Whereas we see philosophers such as Hegel and Ken Wilber (who champions an "up from Eden" view) arguing for the historical progress of humanity, on the other side of the coin, we see those such as Schopenhauer and Gurdjieff, who reject this view. It should be noted, however, although Hegel embraces the upward arc of humanity, he makes it clear that the path to Absolute Knowledge is a rocky one, with temporary downward and sideways steps along the way.

Hegel is most famous for Hegelian dialectic, meaning the triad of thesis, antithesis, and synthesis. What can you say about this in relation to the attainment of Absolute Knowledge?

Dialectic in Western philosophy goes all the way back to Plato. But Hegel, employing the formula "abstract," "negative," "concrete," popularized a new form of dialectic, which was modified into "thesis," "antithesis," "synthesis."

In *The Phenomenology of Spirit*, Hegel uses his dialectic to explain the (postulated by him) workings of the World Spirit through the vehicle of humanity, which is an unwitting instrument for the telos that has been "programmed" into it. Per Hegel, man's consciousness, which seeks to evolve, is designed to function dialectically, meaning that it lurches from one "extreme" (thesis) to another (antithesis) before it finds a "balance" (synthesis). This synthesis then becomes the thesis of another dialectical iteration, resulting in another synthesis, which, in turn, becomes the thesis of yet another dialectical iteration. According to Hegel, it usually takes three such iterations before a final, satisfactory synthesis (balance) is attained.

Hegel's idealism (at least in theory) is wholistic on a worldly level, meaning that the evolutionary dialectical process intersects every area of human life: art, literature, religion, law, economies, social structures, states and communities, human relations, et al. Per the *Routledge Encyclopedia of Philosophy*, Hegel considers the Absolute an "unconditioned reality which is either the spiritual ground of all being or the whole of things considered as a spiritual unity." But Hegel's idealism doesn't provide a methodology to move beyond mundane wholism and unveil the unconditioned Reality, or spiritual Ground, underlying phenomenal reality. His vision of dialectical evolution doesn't transcend change-of-state becoming (mere improvement of man's lot) and yield apprehension of unconditioned Reality, or Absolute Being, without which Absolute Knowledge cannot be attained. His metaphysics is limited to *episteme*, to a philosophy of mind that explains the dynamics of thinking as a means to evolved conditional states, but which doesn't yield *gnosis*, mystical knowledge of the Absolute, of Mind (or God) as Holy Spirit. The World Spirit is not the Holy Spirit, and it is only through the descent of the Holy Spirit

(Divine *Shakti*) into the human soul that the radical leap to *Geist*-realization can be consummated.

Zeitgeistians, Trans-Zeitgeistians, and Geistians

What can you say about Geist-*realization?*

There are three basic levels of civilized humans: *zeitgeistians*, *trans-zeitgeistians*, and *Geistians*. *Zeitgeistians* are the "unwashed" masses. They are unwashed (meaning un-baptized, or un-awakened) both spiritually and socioculturally. They are Matrix-bound, brainwashed to differing degrees by Big Government, Big Education, Big Media, Big Corporations, and Big Religion. As the iconic Zen master Huang Po said, the fur is many and the horns are few. The *zeitgeistians* are the fur.

In contrast to *zeitgeistians*, *trans-zeitgeistians* have "cracked the code" socioculturally and are not "hypnotized" by "the spirit of the times," the sociocultural Matrix that engulfs and conditions the masses. As free-thinking non-conformists, they think outside the box and value truth and liberty more than faith and security. They prefer being disenfranchised outsiders to compromising their values to fit in with the *zeitgeist*.

Geistians are those rare beings, the "horns," who, by virtue of being Blessed by the Holy Spirit, utterly transcend conditional existence when they are immersed in the Divine downpour. Although they are usually also *trans-zeitgeistians*, they understand that Salvation cannot be gained by either transforming or rejecting the mainstream, but only by perpetual abidance in the Divine Stream.

You said that Hegel, whose dialectic is limited to episteme, *doesn't provide the method that yields Spirit-*gnosis. *Do you?*

I've done what Hegel doesn't: provide the dialectical methodology that explains how a *zeitgeistian or a trans-zeitgeistian* can become an unconditioned *Geistian* by uniting his soul (or consciousness) with the Holy Spirit. This dialectical methodology, or spiritual dialectic—thesis (presence), antithesis (absence), synthesis (power)—which yields mystical *gnosis*, will be elaborated in the final chapter [Chapter Sixteen] of *Nonduality and Mind-Only*, which will be titled "Power-of-Now Meditation (Holy Communion)."

Logos Versus Logic

Hegel famously said, "The rational is real, and the real is rational." Is he right?

Decide for yourself. Here are two differing answers that may help you determine if he's right or wrong.

1) No. I contend that whatever exists is real, though the ontological status of existents clearly differs. The real is neither rational nor non-rational; it just is what it is. Rationality is simply the human mind objectively making sense of what it perceives and thinks. It does this through the practice of logic, the non-contradictory identification of the facts of reality. Finally (as quantum theory confirms), "God" does play dice with the universe, and this demonstrates that rationality does not cohere with the chaos we observe in the universe.

2) Yes. Because existence/reality has been "measured out" from the Immeasurable, the Divine Existent, it is inherently rational in nature. Moreover, the Law of Karma (or Cause and Effect) informs us that the universe is "lawful," and thus rational. Finally (as Einstein contended), God does not play dice with the universe: from the Divine viewpoint, there is always only cosmos, a higher rational order behind seeming chaos.

I've seen Hegel's statement interpreted as "God is logic, and logic is God."

For Hegel, the Logos is God's "logic," conveyed through the World Spirit, and played out by man, across the ages, through Hegelian dialectic, via ideas and language. In other words, it (putatively) is Divinely originated evolutionary intelligence operating through the human vehicle in a societal context, with the end goal of Absolute Knowledge.

I don't subscribe to Hegel's conception of the Logos and logic. In particular, although Hegel conflates logic with his dialectic, the two are hardly a match. In fact, his dialectic, for the most part, produces illogic, thereby creating the potential for gross epistemological misuse. Because, unless one postulates a valid thesis/antithesis, the synthesis will have no connection with logic and reality. For example, Hegel's fundamental dialectic—thesis (being), antithesis (nothing), synthesis (becoming)—is an invalid one, because "nothing" is a non-existent with no ontological status.

True logic is, fundamentally, the non-contradictory identification of the facts of reality. And true logic is applied by adhering to Aristotle's three fundamental laws of logic: "A is A" (Identity), "Nothing is both A and non-A" (Non-contradiction), and "Nothing is neither A nor non-A" (Exclusion of the Middle). These laws are not mere hypotheses, but incontrovertible axioms. To deny their validity is to deny the identity of existents and man's cognitive ability to identify these existents and the properties they entail.

In his book *The DIM Hypothesis*, Dr. Leonard Peikoff, the preeminent Ayn Rand scholar, identifies and examines five distinct modes of thought that have dominated four cultural areas during six different Western periods. Peikoff's in-depth analysis makes it clear that when the Aristotelian mode of thinking, which involves "Integration" (the "I" in DIM), is dominant, a civilization flourishes; but when other modes of thought, all of which involve either "Disintegration" (the "D" in DIM) or "Misintegration" (the "M" in DIM), prevail, a civilization decays. The upshot is that the evolvement (or devolvement) of cultures across history is more a reflection of their adherence (or lack thereof) to Aristotelian logic than it is to the effect of Hegelian dialectic. And, as history makes clear, the epitome of the Aristotelian mode of thinking is the Enlightenment, the acme of Western civilization.

So does Aristotelian logic represent the Logos?

The Logos is the incarnate Word/Christ/Son/Self/Buddha, meaning nondual, pure Consciousness itself. Logic, on the other hand, is dualistic, involving "impure," or thought-impli-cated, consciousness. One could say that the Logos, enacted by a yogi or a mystic, is an act of onto-logic, of thought-free Self-expression; whereas (Aristotelian) logic, applied by a logician, is the thought-full act of identifying the facts of reality.

Dialectical Marxism

Karl Marx took Hegel's spiritual idea of dialectic and converted it into a materialist one. Instead of a dialectic devoted to man's spiritual evolution, Marx, and the Marxians who followed him, applied, and continue to apply, Hegelian dialectic to the Godless goal of utopian socialism. The result has been an un-mitigated disaster of epic proportions, with mega-millions of people dying in the name of, and under the thumb of, Marxist-inspired revolutions and governments. And now, cultural Marxists, practitioners of the religion of "Wokeism," continue to employ invalid Hegelian dialectic in their impossible quest for "social justice," meaning DEI, the misguided and societally destructive ideals of diversity, equity, and inclusion.

I know more than a little about Marxism (including cultural Marxism); I studied it directly under the iconic Herbert Marcuse at UCSD. As an ignorant and naive 18-year-old freshman, I bought into the "repressive tolerance" preached by Dr. Marcuse and actively took part in on-campus demonstrations aimed at shutting down free speech. But by my junior year, I realized that Marcuse's playbook for the New Left (which is now being implemented by cancel-culture leftists) was really fascist, and I was on my way to becoming a right-libertarian.

The fundamental dialectic of Marxism—Dialectical Materialism—is an invalid one, and some staunch proponents of Marxism even grudgingly admit this. The idea that the exploited, poor working class represents the thesis, the exploiting rich capitalist class the antithesis, and (after the revolution), the rich, class-free Communist social order the synthesis, is laughable to anyone with intelligence who has studied history. And the procession of "creative" new, but invalid, dialectics by the "woke" neo-Marxists has further exposed the shortcomings and potential misuse of Hegelian dialectic. In short, this misuse of Hegelian dialectic by the left represents the antithesis of Aristotelian logic and Enlightenment values; hence it portends the destruction of Western civilization.

Anyone interested in Hegelian dialectic and the history of its application (really misapplication) by classical Marxism, and then cultural Marxism, should check out the New Discourses YouTube channel, which features the brilliant James Lindsay, the foremost contemporary critic and deconstructor of Marxism in all its forms, past and present. I especially enjoy listening to Lindsay expose the fascist ideas underpinning the putatively "liberating" neo-Marxist ideology popularized by my old professor, Dr. Marcuse.

You've just reamed Hegelian dialectic, yet you employ it not only in your Electrical Spiritual Paradigm (ESP), but also sociopolitically [in the article "Buddhist Politics 501," which can be found in Chapter Eleven or Googled online], with individualism / capitalism as your thesis and statism / socialism as your antithesis. How do you justify this?

Simple: Hegelian dialectic is a tool, which, like fire, can be used "lawfully" and constructively, or "unlawfully" and destructively. Unlike the Marxists and neo-Marxists, I employ it not only "lawfully" and constructively, but also innovatively.

Okay, a final question: What can you say about Hegel's idealism in relation to nonduality and Mind-Only?

Hegel understood that the manifest world is a reflection of unmanifest Mind, which alone is ultimately Real. He rightly held that manifest existence derives from and is subsumed by the unmanifest Existent, which implies nonduality. While I'm critical of some aspects of his philosophic idealism, I applaud his inventive effort to explain the "phenomenology of Spirit," and aim to build upon parts of it.

CHAPTER NINE

The Prismatic Paradigm, Part 1

An Integral Mind / Manifestation Consideration

In our talks, we've considered unmanifest Mind (or God) in relation to manifest existence in the contexts of the *Lankavatara Sutra*, Huang Po's Zen, Kashmir Shaivism, Kabbalah, and Hegel's *Phenomenology of Spirit*. Now, I'll attempt an integral Mind/manifestation consideration that combines parts of our previous discussions while adding a few new wrinkles. First, a confession: Because I'm a philosophical generalist involved in multiple projects, I have not, at this time, fully developed my Prismatic Paradigm. I consider it a work in progress that I will upgrade over time, and if at some point I'm satisfied with a "finished product," I'll publish it. And if I never manage to complete an upgrade, others are welcome to attempt one.

Why publish it now (as it's presented in our talks) when it's still in an embryonic stage?

Given that I'm probably the only living mystic-philosopher who could think up such a theosophical model (which I think many will appreciate, even if it's raw), I'm moved to do so now because I'm 73, and men in my family line don't live particularly long.

After finishing my last book, *Radical Dzogchen*, my plan was to begin work on a Kabbalah text. At the same time I was contemplating the theosophical Kabbalah and the Tree of Life, I was also reading books and watching YouTube videos on nonduality and metaphysical idealism. As I considered what I was reading and watching, I realized that little of it impressed me, much of it I disagreed with, and that I could provide a deeper, more integral paradigm.

Moreover, in a book that provided a paradigm elaborating nonduality and Mind-Only through the prism of reality, I could include a Kabbalah chapter that would serve as the basis for my Kabbalah text. Hence, I would effectively be killing two birds with one stone.

What I'm going to do now, in a series of discussions, is (1) reconsider Kashmir Shaivism (KS), Kabbalah, and phenomenology of Spirit, (2) attempt to creatively combine them, and (3) construct a new Kabbalistic Tree of Life in the process.

My goal in these discussions won't be to fully elaborate this new Tree of Life (a task that will be continued in my forthcoming Kabbalah book), but to apply the ideas behind the Tree to foster greater insight into the theme we're now focusing on: nonduality and Mind-Only through the prism of reality. We'll start our series of discussions with Kashmir Shaivism.

Creation as a Refractive Theophany

I resonate with Kashmir Shaivism's five-fold "Divine Order" as a description/imagination of Mind's (or God's, or *Siva's*) fundamental pre-creation "activity." *Siva* as *Shakti*, His inseparable Consort, asserts His absolute sovereignty and power as *Iccha-Shakti*, His will to create. Then, as *Jnana-Shakti*, He employs His infinite wisdom to "plan" His creation. Finally, as *Kriya-Shakti*, He, the Immeasurable One, "measures Himself out" as creation, while "hiding Himself" in His theophany.

This fivefold pre-genesis paradigm has *Siva*, or *Cit*, as Mind, *Shakti* as Mind's Energy, *Iccha* as Mind's Will, *Jnana* as Mind's Knowledge, and *Kriya* as Mind's Creativity. Rather than a static Absolute, as Advaita Vedanta has it, Kashmir Shaivism maintains that the Supreme is not just *Cit*, but also *Shakti*, operative prior to and post manifestation.

The KS pre-manifestation description trumps Kabbalah's because it explains Mind's transition from acausal God to creator God. And rather than, untenably, describing creation via a muddled cataclysmic act (the shattering of defective vessels), as Kabbalah does, KS provides us with a copacetic depiction of *Maya* as *Siva*'s (or Mind's) Self-organized descent into Self-limitation and division. So, in my Tree of Life [Diagram 3], I employ KS's "Divine Order" to represent *Siva's*/Mind's pre-genesis activity.

In his The Doctrine of Recognition, A Translation of Pratyabhijnahrdayam with an Introduction and Notes, *Jaideva Singh writes, "The Universe is nothing but an opening out* (unmesa) *or expansion of the Supreme or rather of the Supreme as* Sakti [Shakti]."

Exactly. And because I champion this view, while the current big-name promoters of nonduality and metaphysical idealism don't, I feel moved to counter their static Consciousness-Only arguments by providing a dynamical Spiritual (or *Shakti*-based) explanation of the descent of the Divine Mind into, and as, manifestation.

So, from the KS perspective, what happens when the universe opens out from the Supreme?

The Supreme's first act as "Creator God," *Kriya-Shakti*, is to conceal and limit Himself as *Maya*. The immediate products of *Maya tattva* are the five *Kancukas* (coverings), which, in our earlier consideration of KS, I described as follows: *Kala* contracts/cloaks sovereign power; *Vidya* contracts/cloaks omniscience; *Raga* contracts/cloaks bliss; *Kaala* contracts/cloaks timelessness; and *Nityati* contracts/cloaks spacelessness. *Maya*, in the KS system, does not mean "illusion," but phenomenal reality—manifest space-time existents as contracted/cloaked *Siva*, who, for sport, created, and hid Himself in, the cosmos.

The Divine Order

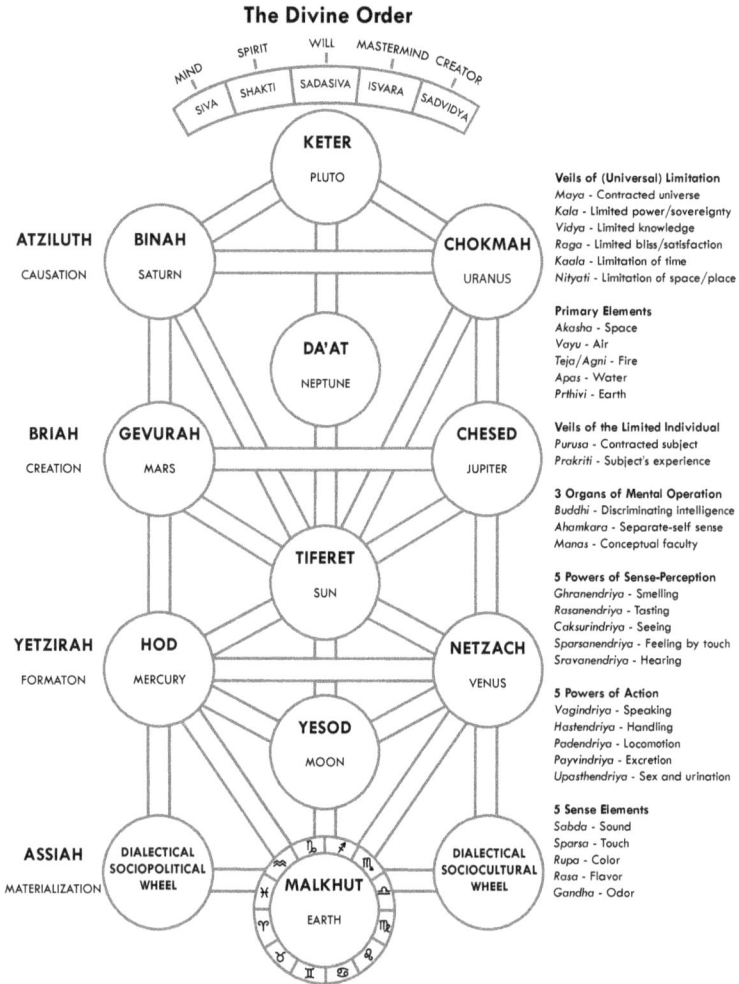

Diagram 3. The 3-Dimensional Tree of Life

We've now enumerated the first 11 *tattvas* (which constitute the five-fold "Divine Order," *Maya*, and the five *Kancukas*). From this point, I'm going to deviate from the KS *tattva* order by placing the *Mahabhutas* (*tattvas* 32-36, per KS) as 12-16 in my order. In our previous KS discussion, I provided the rationale for inserting the *Mahabhutas* ahead of *Purusa* and *Prakriti*, and I'll now summarily repeat what I said.

The fact that *Maya tattva* contracts/cloaks spacelessness and timelessness (meaning spaceless, timeless God, or Mind, or *Siva*) signifies that, as *Maya-Shakti*, God/Mind/*Siva* has morphed into the ether (*Akasha*), the all-pervading space element (or "substance"), and that separate, created existents (or objects) moving/changing successively in that ethereal space results in time. Without the ether and the four fundamental elements that stem from it—fire, earth, air, water—forming a substrate, there can be no further creation, meaning no living *Purusas* to experience their *Prakriti* and embody the remainder of the *tattvas* in the KS hierarchy.

So, instead of the "five gross elements" (*Mahabhutas*), the "*tattvas* of materiality" (32-36) in the standard KS schema, we now have the "five great elements"— *Akasha* (space), *Vayu* (air), *Teja* or *Agni* (fire), *Apas* (water), and *Prthivi* (earth)—as *tattvas* 12-16, with *Purusa* and *Prakriti* now, respectively, as *tattvas* 17 and 18.

Purusa and *Prakriti* are classified as the "*tattvas* of the limited individual." As I stated in our previous KS discussion, *Purusa* is the individual subject, contracted into a point (*anu*) of self-awareness in the midst of Infinity. It is the Divine Person, *Siva*, cloaked as an empirical person/experient. *Prakriti* is the objective material (gross and subtle) manifestation experienced by an individual *Purusa*. Hence, in contrast to Samkhya philosophy, which equates *Prakriti* with the total dynamic elemental manifestation, a.k.a. "nature," KS "personalizes" "impersonal" *Prakriti*.

I'll now complete our enumeration of the *tattvas* by restating what I said in our previous KS discussion (only changing the numbers of the *tattvas* to agree with our new order). *Tattvas* 19 (*Buddhi*), 20 (*Ahamkara*), and 21 (*Manas*) are called the "*tattvas* of mental operation." *Buddhi* is the intellect, the discriminating intelligence of the mind. It is sometimes referred to as the "higher mind." *Ahamkara* is the separate-self sense, or contracted I-consciousness. *Manas* is the mind that processes and mediates sensory information and habit-tendencies. It is sometimes referred to as the "lower mind."

The now final *tattvas* (after our elevation of the *Mahabhutas* ahead of *Purusa* and *Prakriti*) are those of "sensible experience" (22-36). These *tattvas*, which are products of *Ahamkara*, are the "five powers of sense-perception" (*Jnanendriyas* or *Buddhindriyas*): smelling (*ghranendriya*), tasting (*rasanendriya*), seeing (*caksurindriya*), feeling by touch (*sparsanendriya*), hearing (*sravanendriya*); the "five powers of action" (*Karmendriyas*): speaking (*vagindriya*), handling (*hastendriya*), locomotion (*padendriya*), excreting (*payvindriya*), sexual action and restfulness (*upasthendriya*); and the "five primary elements of perception"(*Tanmatras*): sound-as-such (*sabda-tanmatra*), touch-as-such (*sparsa-tanmatra*), color-as-such (*rupa-tanmatra*), flavor-as-such (*rasa-tanmatra*), odor-as-such (*gandha-tanmatra*).

What more can you say about the tattvas?

Plenty, but since our current series of talks focuses on the broad-based themes of nonduality and Mind-Only, rather than on the specific subject matter of KS, deep delving into the *tattvas* will have to wait another day. Moreover, the new Kabbalistic Tree of Life that I have "cobbled together" is not a

finished product, but a work in progress that I just happened
to concoct in the course of our discussions. Hence, in the process of this work, we'll revisit and further consider the *tattvas*.

CHAPTER TEN

The Prismatic Paradigm, Part 2

Let me know if I'm clear on your 3-Dimensional Tree of Life [Diagram 3]. You have God/Mind (which Kashmir Shaivism personifies as Siva), prior to genesis, "planning/preparing" manifestation through the five-fold Divine Order. Then Kriya-Shakti *(the fifth and final of the unmanifest Divine Order* tattvas*), as its first act, as willed by Siva, manifests as* Maya *and the five* Kancukas, *thereby contracting/cloaking God/Mind by seemingly reducing and limiting Him, the Illimitable spaceless-timeless One, to a space-time universe inhabited with sentient and insentient existents, with man alone, at least on planet Earth, as the designated agent/existent assigned with the task of uniting Heaven (Mind) and Earth. And then, at the bottom of the Tree, you have the dialectical sociopolitical and sociocultural wheels, which you'll begin considering in our next discussion.*

Not bad. I can tell that you've been contemplating my diagram, which (for those who will be reading this), I termed the "3-Dimensional Tree of Life" because it combines astrology, Kashmir Shaivism, and quasi-Hegelian phenomenology into a new Kabbalistic paradigm.

Let me know if I've got this right. I see the non-Divine (or manifest) tattvas on the right side of the diagram as representing the involutional continuum of Maya *directly through the agency of man. The central core of the Tree, the Sefirot, which you conflate with the planets of our solar system [which, in astrology, include the Sun and the Moon], represents the stepped-down descent of Divine Influence through the refractive medium of cosmic agents (planets), each of which has rulership over a particular domain or dimension of human earthly existence.*

Well said! Combining the KS *tattva* system with the classical Sefirotic/astrologic Tree of Life clearly serves to upgrade the Tree as a theosophical chart. That said, I'm sure many traditionalists will recoil in response to my "creative" redrawing of the Kabbalistic Tree.

I'm also sure that many into Hindu Vedic astrology will not be happy with my rejection of the sidereal (mutable constellation-based) zodiac they embrace and my allegiance to the tropical (immutable solar-system-based) zodiac, which most Western astrologers endorse. Here [below] for those who will be reading our exchange is a brief comparison of the two zodiacs (excerpted from the article "Sidereal and Tropical Zodiacs" at universallifechurch.org):

> Both sidereal and tropical zodiac systems typically use the same 12 astrological signs, with the Sun taking 30 to 31 days to transit each sign. The key difference between the two is their starting points. Astrological years begin with zero degrees Aries, but tropical astrology always places this point at the spring equinox. Sidereal systems place zero degrees Aries at the [subjective] point where the Sun actually starts transiting through the constellation of Aries. That's why sidereal Aries currently starts [circa] April 15 instead of March 21.
>
> Why is there such a huge difference in starting dates? It's because sidereal systems account for equinox precession. As seen from Earth, the constellations' positions in our night skies drift westward [about 1 degree each 72 years]. This drift results from the movement of Earth's rotational axis, which also gives us our north and south

geographic poles. Solar and lunar gravitational forces pull on our planet, causing the poles' locations to shift in relation to the stars' positions. But from Earth, it looks like the stars themselves are moving.

In short, the single tropical zodiac is based on the Earth-Sun relationship, which is objective, while the various, differing sidereal systems depend on our planet's relationship to the stars, which is subjective. (As the website masteringthezodiac.com puts it, "Sidereal astrology uses the visible sky for its zodiac system. Aries begins where it is visible. Since this is subjective, there are many different forms of sidereal.") Given that the Earth-Sun relationship is stable and objective, whereas the Earth-stars relationship is not, it is only the tropical zodiac that represents perennial and unchanging aspects.

Because the Kabbalistic Tree of Life has nothing to do with the subjective, ever-changing Earth-stars relationship, and everything to do with the objective, constant Earth-Sun-Planet relationships, it is clearly compatible with the tropical zodiac, but not the sidereal. And to emphasize the relationship of the Sun and the planets with the Earth, I have, in my diagram, placed a zodiac "belt" around Earth/*Malkhut*. This signifies that humans on planet Earth receive planetary (including solar and lunar) energies/influences that are modified/"filtered" through the twelve zodiac signs.

An individual's "soul-matrix" (the composite of psychical seed tendencies that "sprouts" as his/her mind and emotions) reflects the planetary "gestalt" (as "filtered" through the twelve zodiac signs) at the moment he/she was born. And a natal astrology chart, a diagram of this "filtered" planetary gestalt, provides a map of his/her psychical (karmic) structures, which an astrologer deciphers.

It seems that one must become an astrologer in order to deeply grok the theosophical Kabbalah.

Yes, and that holds true not only for Kabbalah, but also Hermeticism and occultism. In the case of the Kabbalistic Tree of Life, one cannot deeply grok the Sefirot without a deep understanding of astrology, because, as I've made clear, the Sefirot are analogues for the planets (which, in astrological nomenclature, include the Sun and the Moon).

Likewise, one cannot deeply (or occultly) grok oneself, others, or interpersonal relationships sans astrology. That said, I must emphasize that, whereas astrological chart erection is a science (in the sense that it is based on astronomical information), chart interpretation is an art; and the depth and accuracy of interpretations can vary significantly, depending on the training and ability of the astrologer.

In our previous discussions on the theosophical Kabbalah, you went into extensive detail on the Tree of Life and the prismatic function of the planets. What more can you add to your previous discourse on the subject?

Our previous discussions on Kabbalah were more extensive and detailed than those on Kashmir Shaivism and the phenomenology of Spirit because they served to lay the groundwork for my forthcoming Kabbalah text. At this point, it makes no sense for me to repeat all the same arguments and explanations and then expand upon them, because to properly do so would take a book, which is next on my agenda after *Nonduality and Mind-Only* is completed and published.

Alex Jones describes our world as a "prison planet," controlled by New World Order, "Great Reset" globalists, most notably Klaus Schwab [who retired from his post as head of the WEF in May 2024] and George

Soros. But you describe it as a "prism planet," in effect controlled, or at least greatly influenced, by the planets in our solar system.

Alex is right, and so am I. And when we next consider the third "leg" of my Prismatic Paradigm, which pertains to a phenomenology of Spirit, we'll address the sociopolitical ideologies and ideas that permeate, and transcend, the zeitgeist, including those of "conspiracy theorists" such as Alex Jones.

CHAPTER ELEVEN

Beyond *The Phenomenology of Spirit,* Part 2

My Phenomenology Story

When, in 1971, as a 19-year-old sophomore at UC San Diego, I began to sour on Marxism, my intellectual focus turned to existentialism. Having specialized in Albert Camus's writings as a senior in high school, I was now motivated to delve deeply into Jean-Paul Sartre's works, as well as those of other existentialists. I took a sociology class taught by Professor Stanford Lyman (author of *A Sociology of the Absurd*) on existential phenomenology, and I was so taken with the subject that I decided to major in sociology, while minoring in philosophy. But the best laid plans of men (especially college students) often go awry, and by my junior year I had lost all interest in both sociology and existentialism, as I became infatuated with Eastern spirituality. I stayed in school to avoid the Viet Nam War draft and got my degree in sociology, but my life was now devoted to my "journey to the East."

In my study of phenomenology at UCSD, I read Husserl, Heidegger, Merleau-Ponty, and others (and I had already studied Hegel under Dr. Herbert Marcuse), but once I graduated, I didn't look at another phenomenology text until I read Avi Sion's excellent *Phenomenology: Basing Knowledge on Appearance* about seven years ago. Sion's book got me thinking, and I decided that at some point I wanted to apply my philosophic insights to the subject of phenomenology; and that's what I'm now doing in our talks.

Very interesting. So now, in our talks [between late 2023 and early 2024], you're going to present an innovative spiritual version of phenomenology.

Only as it pertains to Spirit's dialectical workings in the sphere of mundane reality. At some point in my writing career, I will focus on the phenomenology of Spirit as it pertains to the esoteric "mechanics" of spiritual Awakening, but not now. Rather, a la Hegel, I'm going to center my discourse on dialectical phenomenology as it applies to understanding the dualistic "mechanics" of Spirit's workings through the zeitgeist. But rather than provide a historical analysis, my breakdown will focus on the current sociopolitical and sociocultural landscape, considering it in the context of the fundamental polar principles that constitute the two "phenomenological wheels" at the base of my 3-Dimensional Tree of Life (see Diagram 3, and for the breakdown of the two wheels into their dialectical components/oppositions, see Diagram 4).

Because Kashmir Shaivism's 36 *tattvas* and the Sefirotic/planetary Tree provide the most sophisticated schemas of the hierarchical "bridge" between God (or Mind) and man that I'm aware of, I chose them (in upgraded form) to constitute the core of my Tree of Life. I then added a "third dimension," the dialectical, quasi-Hegelian "phenomenological wheels," to complete my 3-Dimensional Tree of Life Diagram.

The Dialectical Sociopolitical Wheel

As you can see (in Diagram 4), the first wheel, which I've termed the "Dialectical Sociopolitical Wheel," has two dialectical oppositions: capitalism vs. socialism and individualism vs. statism. Because my book *Zen Mind, Thinker's Mind* includes a chapter— "Buddhist Politics 501"—that elucidates these oppositions, rather than (less cogently) restating my explanation of these dialectical poles, I'll simply read [present] the entire chapter, riff on the current sociopolitical milieu (while including some of my other sociopolitical writings), and conclude by applying Hegelian dialectic to analyze the current left (socialism / statism) vs. right (capitalism / individualism) opposition.

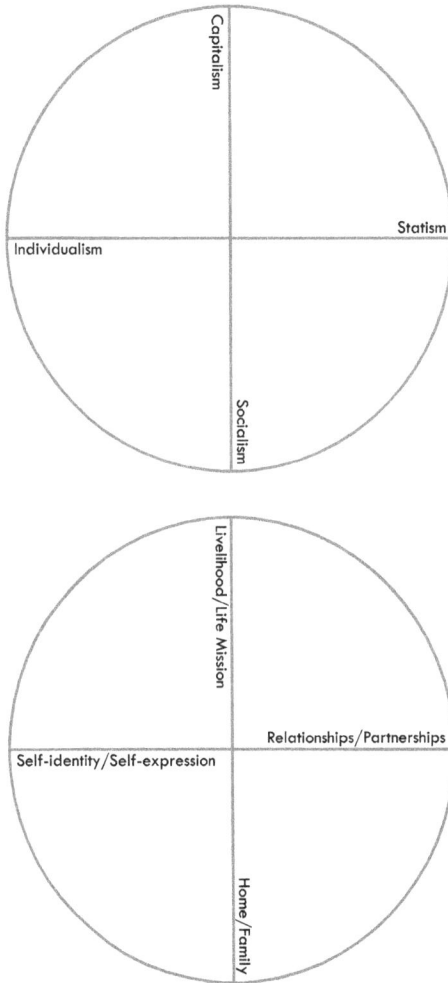

Diagram 4. The Dialectical Sociopolitical and Sociocultural Wheels

BUDDHIST POLITICS 501

According to the Pew Research Center's party affiliation among Buddhists by political ideology survey in 2014 (http://www.pewforum.org/religious-landscape-study/compare/political-ideology/by/party-affiliation/among/religious-tradition/buddhist/), 12% of American Buddhists identify themselves as conservatives, 32% as moderates, 54% as liberals, and 2% "don't know." There is little reason to doubt the veracity of this survey because other such surveys provide similar results.

Left-wing Buddhists not only outnumber right-wingers by more than a 4/1 ratio, but many of them are now devoted to combining Buddhism with a "progressive" political agenda. At his blog Hardcore Zen (hardcorezen.info), Brad Warner comments on this phenomenon:

> What bugs me is when it appears that liberal, left-leaning Buddhists are trying to mix Buddhism with their political agenda in precisely the same way people like Pat Robertson mix Christianity with their conservative political agenda. This just makes us all look bad to everyone except lefty types who already agree with whatever cause is being espoused. Nobody is going to be convinced to change their views on militarism or global warming because they saw a photo of a bunch of weirdos in costumes they associate with cult members holding a banner outside of the White House. It is an exercise in vanity, which can only serve to help entrench people's previously established views.

In contrast to Brad Warner, I have no problem with Buddhists pushing a political agenda; I just have a problem with their "liberal" agenda, which is contrary to what the Buddha taught. This liberal agenda is based on the forceful (socialistic) transference of wealth, which amounts to theft, a violation of a fundamental

Buddhist tenet. At her blog ThoughtCo. (thoughtco.com), Barbara O'Brien comments on this:

> The second Buddhist precept often is translated "do not steal." Some Buddhist teachers prefer "practice generosity." A more literal translation of the early Pali texts is "I undertake the precept to refrain from taking that which is not given."

Because this theft of money entails force and violence—the government will imprison you if you don't pay what they demand—the left-wing agenda of wealth transference not only violates the second Buddhist precept, but also the first: non-killing, which extends to include non-violence. As the website Clear Vision (www. clear-vision.org) puts it:

> Buddhists have always interpreted this [the first] precept to mean, not merely a prohibition of murder, but of all kinds of violence against human beings and animals.

What left-wingers fail to grasp is the difference between voluntary communal activity and coercive statist socialism. While the former is non-violent, the latter isn't. The State typically devolves into an authoritarian Leviathan that fascistically and Orwellianly dictates how people live their lives and spend their money. It becomes a monolithic corruptocracy, wherein politicians, bought off by big-money special interests, enact legislation that delimits the (putatively guaranteed) constitutional rights of the country's citizens, who, brainwashed by public schools, left-wing universities, and the mainstream media, willingly obey, and even worship, their Big Government masters.

Because American Buddhists are big on compassion, on helping the poor and needy, they typically support government aid programs such as welfare, food stamps, and housing subsidies. But these programs, over the decades, have proved to be an abysmal failure, and rather than helping the downtrodden, they have, in effect, enslaved them, making them dependent and dysfunctional. For example, in 1960, 80% of black children were born into two-parent families, but now, a half century after the War on Poverty was begun under President Lyndon Johnson, that figure is down to 30%. In other words, the welfare state, initiated by Johnson in 1964, has decimated the black nuclear family. It has done so by incentivizing black women to have lots of kids sans a husband, because the more such children a woman has, the larger her welfare check will be. The black man, meanwhile, divorced from a supportive family structure, often turns to crime and ends up in prison. But mindless left-wingers continue to waste billions of taxpayers' dollars on social programs that not only don't work, but exacerbate the problem. Cities such as Detroit and Chicago are sobering examples of the urban plight perpetuated by the failed social programs of the left over the past fifty years.

The modern left has essentially lost its mind, degenerating from classical liberalism (which virtually mirrors modern right-wing libertarianism) into a postmodern potpourri of agendas that derive from classical and cultural Marxism. These include, but aren't limited to, anti-capitalism, political correctness, censorship of the right, and oppressor/oppressed power politics (which focus on class, gender, and racial distinctions). Fundamentally, the modern left is about authoritarian social engineering enforced by a quasi-fascist Big-Brother State.

The "Right-Wing" Solution

If modern left-wing politics, which forcefully and violently sacrifices the putatively sovereign individual to the dictates of the State, isn't the political solution for Buddhists, then is "right-wing" politics? Not if one considers the mainstream Republican

Party to represent such politics; for, in truth, their political agenda differs only marginally from that of the Democrats. A true right-wing, or true Republican, agenda would be about re-establishing America as a true constitutional republic, wherein the constitutional rights of individuals have primacy over, rather than being subordinated to, the dictates of mob-rule democracy, wherein the brainwashed masses are able to vote them away.

In my opinion, the sociopolitical ideology that best reflects Buddhist ethics is right (or right-wing) libertarianism, which subscribes to the credo of self-ownership and the non-initiation of force. This credo or ethos perfectly meshes with the Buddha's vision of personal, interpersonal, and social morality, exemplified by his five precepts. Although libertarianism (which developed in the 1950s) is often categorized as "extreme right-wing," in reality, it closely resembles nineteenth-century classical (or neo-classical) liberalism, as opposed to modern social ("progressive") liberalism.

Integral Dialectical Politics

I think the best way to explain the relation between right-wing libertarianism and left-wing social liberalism is via Hegelian dialectic, wherein the former (which represents the pole of individualism/capitalism) is the thesis, and the latter (which represents the pole of statism/socialism) is the antithesis. Because individualism/capitalism *subsumes* statism/socialism (meaning the former allows for the latter, but not vice-versa), the synthesis that results is an individualist/capitalist system that *sublates* (or subordinates but preserves) the State and allows for *voluntary* collectivism. In other words, in a moral, or "integral," society, the State still exists, but its function is limited to providing national security and protecting and preserving individual rights (including property rights).

Voluntary socialism or collectivism is fine. In an individualist-capitalist system, individuals can freely form communes or collectives if they so desire. But in a statist-socialist system, you cannot set up a John Galt-type capitalist community that is independent of the State. Big Brother will insist on regulating your town and taxing your townspeople.

The most persecuted minority is the individual, and the only social system that frees individuals from the dictates of special interest groups (which typically seek to divide and conquer through the weapons of class, gender, and racial distinctions) is laissez-faire (or free-market) capitalism. Free-market capitalism is based on the "trader principle," wherein independent agents voluntarily, rather than coercively, agree to exchange goods, services, and monies. This social system is the only one that morally coheres with the Buddha's five precepts and prescribed practice of right livelihood.

If "liberal" (really liberal-fascist) special-interest groups want to implement their social-engineering programs (which amount to dictatorial theft and control), instead of doing so through the agency of the domineering State, they should do so by setting up their own private Marxist or quasi-Marxist collectives and communes, rather than by forcing those of us true to Buddhist principles to participate in their socialist agenda.

The Evils of Democratic Governments

More than coincidentally, perhaps, while seated on the john during a bathroom break in the midst of writing this article, I just happened to grab a book, *The Tibetan Book of the Great Liberation* by W.Y. Evans-Wentz, from a box of many, open it to a random page, and see the apropos quote below. I took this as a sign that I was to include it in my article, so here it is:

Plato, the greatest of Greek Sages, spent many years in an attempt to define Justice, or what the Hindu Sages call *Dharma*. He recognized the evils of democratic governments, wherein it is not the right, or justice, which always prevails, but the will of the philosophically untrained vulgar majority; and that it is fallacious to assume that the minority are always wrong. It is with these conditions in view that the *Gurus* teach that the great man is he who differs in every thought and action from the multitude. Accordingly, it has ever been the lone pioneers of thought, the sowers of the seed of new ages, the Princes of Peace, rather than the Lords of War, and the minorities (who may be the disciples of the Sages), that have suffered martyrdom and social ostracism at the hands of the majority, who impose their standards of good and evil upon the helpless minority.

It is therefore very unwise to accept without question, as is nowadays customary in many modern states where sound moral principles prevail, the verdict of the people, whether expressed by a jury in a court of law or through the ballot box, as to what is justice, right or wrong, good or evil. So long as mankind are more selfish than altruistic, the majority are unfit to dominate the minority, who may be much the better citizens. As both Plato and the Wise Men of the East teach, the democratic-majority standard of judgment as to what is moral and immoral conduct is unreliable.

The fundamental point that well-meaning Buddhist Democrats need to grok is that, in a moral society, the majority has no right to vote away the sacrosanct rights of the individual, and sacrifice him or her to the normative dictates of the collective. For example, the government should not be able to outlaw drugs, gambling, prostitution, and other victimless "crimes." It should not be able to force individuals to buy medical insurance, pay income tax, or vaccinate their children. Those who, a la Hillary Clinton, believe that "it takes a village" should realize that participation in the "village" must be voluntary, not compulsory. This is so because America, first and foremost, is a constitutional republic, and only secondarily a democracy, which means that the democratic (voting) process should be limited to electing officials (or representatives) and should not infringe upon the constitutional rights of citizens. When Buddhist Democrats understand this, and its relation to what the Buddha taught regarding ethics, they will understand Right Politics.

I like the Right Politics you plug in your article, but are you advocating anarchy?

No. First off, the term anarchy does not imply violence. Anarchy simply means anti-statism; so it can be entirely peaceful, as libertarian anarchists envision it. But I'm not an anarchist. Rather, I favor a minimal state, because I fear that a stateless country or society would devolve into a dystopian "jungle," wherein violent war-like gangs mercilessly compete for dominance and control.

What I'm advocating is sovereignty. If everyone is guaranteed sovereignty, then no one can legally interfere with the sovereignty or individual rights (including property rights) of others. Sovereignty does not include the right to initiate force against another person or his property. But the State initiates force against citizens by arresting them for victimless "crimes" (drugs, prostitution, gambling, etc.) and for not paying taxes ("protection money" to the "Mafia State"). Moreover, it initiates force (theft) against them when it engages in "quantitative easing" (inflationary money printing), which devalues their dollars. Those against the initiation of force and violence (which would include all true spiritual gurus/teachers) should be outspoken critics, or even outright enemies, of today's Mafia State. But, unfortunately, very few spiritual gurus/teachers understand the anti-spiritual nature and function of the Marxist Mafia State.

You wrote your article a few years ago. What can you say about it now?

A lot has changed since I wrote it, so it doesn't do justice to the depraved depths that the left has sunk to in the interim. Under the dictatorial rulership of the Biden regime, America has devolved into a quasi-Marxist-Fascist banana republic, wherein the uber-corrupt Democrat Party employs government agencies (most notably the FBI, CIA, DOJ, NSA, and IRS) to target and harass its political opposition (especially Donald Trump and the MAGA movement) for pseudo-crimes, while its own egregious and treasonous crimes remain exempt from legal consequences. And because the current Democrat Party subscribes to the Communist dictum "the end justifies the means," it freely and shamelessly engages in election interference/rigging in its attempt to consummate a Marxist revolution. The fact that, in order to influence the 2020 election, 51 former U.S. intelligence agents conspired with the Biden campaign to falsely claim that emails on Hunter Biden's laptop were Russian disinformation, tells us how corrupt the Democrat-controlled Deep State is.

Virtually every policy the Democrats now enact, or seek to enact, reeks of insanity and/or tyranny. It's as if they are intent on destroying America as a constitutional republic, as a beacon of liberty and equality. And this destruction is most evident in cities that have gone full-on "progressive" left. If you want to see what a future progressive, or "woke," America would look like, check out the devastation that "Wokeism," the secular religion of the left, has wrought in Seattle, Portland, New York, and San Francisco. Donald Trump nailed it when he said, "Everything woke turns to shit."

*Yep, everything they champion—illegal immigration, mail-in voting/
no voter ID, defunding the police, student loan forgiveness, reparations
for slavery, central bank digital currency, social credit scores, limitless
(bankrupting) money printing/spending, income tax on unrealized
capital gains, mandatory vaccines/lockdowns, censorship/cancel culture, a dystopian Disinformation Governance Board, climate-change
hysteria, sex-change operations for children, allowing biological males
to compete in female sports, et al.—bespeaks of insanity and tyranny.
It's as if the left has lost their mind and moral compass.*

Exactly. The only thing progressive about the "progressive"
left is their brain rot and immorality. Consider that every
Democrat congressman, all 200 + of them, voted to allow biological males to compete as females in women's sports. Only
someone afflicted with the libtard virus would seek to legally
enable such madness.

Leftist thinking, as exemplified by the said unanimous vote to
allow men to compete as women, is hivemind thinking, brainless conformity. Why isn't there a single current Washington
Democrat who qualifies as a true statesman, meaning an independent, incisive thinker-speaker? While the Republican
Party is blessed with multiple impressive statesmen (such as
Rand Paul, Ted Cruz, and Josh Hawley), the Democrat Party
is teeming with total idiots (such as Joe Biden, Kamala Harris,
Nancy Pelosi, Adam Schiff, Maxine Waters, and AOC), who
are not only stupid, but ineloquent.

The fact that not a single Democrat congressman or sena-
tor has identified the banana republic kangaroo court cases
against Trump for what they are—fascist anti-democratic
measures to prevent him from becoming President again—
bespeaks of their collective, lobotomized Marxist mentality.

The libtard virus has taken over their brains, sucking them dry of intelligence and integrity.

What's amazing is how even "the best and the brightest," the elite minds at our top universities, have also fallen victim to the libtard virus.

Very true. Entrepreneur and creator of Valuetainment (a YouTube channel with 5 million + subscribers), Patrick Bet-David, a right-libertarian, attended a Harvard Business seminar in 2016. Per Bet-David, when attendees were asked who they supported for president in the then-forthcoming election, all hands but his were raised in support of "Crooked Hillary," the epitome of a libtard criminal.

The problem with leftist intellectuals is that most of them are hubris-bloated elitists who want to dictate how the rest of us should think, talk, act, and vote. A good example of this is Noam Chomsky, who many, laughably, consider a libertarian. Chomsky is a Marxist who believes that people (such as automobile factory workers) who work for a big company should be granted part ownership of that company. Chomsky supports the tyrannical Biden regime, and he vociferously argued for draconian COVID vaccine mandates and lockdowns—anti-constitutional measures to isolate the unvaccinated from society.

Another prominent leftist "intellectual" infected with the libtard virus is "Soapbox" Sam Harris. Sam "the Sham" (a pseudo-thinker masquerading as a sagely philosopher) not only suffers from 4th-stage Trump Derangement Syndrome so severe that he considers Donald Trump a worse (more immoral) person than Osama Bin Laden, he also supported the actions of the 51 former U.S. intelligence agents who falsely claimed that the emails on Hunter Biden's laptop were Russian disinformation. As a prototypical authoritarian elitist, Sam has no problem with election influencing/rigging, so long as it guarantees that the candidate he KNOWS is best for us lowly plebs gets elected. And, of course, Sam supported the same tyrannical COVID policies as Chomsky.

Yet another example of a big-name intellectual infected with the libtard virus is world-famous Harvard professor Howard Gardner. It's no coincidence that Howard's last name is the same as mine—he's my cousin! After I had finished and self-published *Zen Mind, Thinker's Mind: New Perspectives on Buddhadharma, Consciousness*, and *Awakening* (in 2022), I contacted Howard and provided him with a copy. Howard's many books are primarily about mind, so I assumed that he'd be familiar with Buddhist theories of mind; but, to my surprise, he pleaded ignorance regarding Buddhism. In return for my book, he sent me a copy of his latest: *A Synthesizing Mind: A Memoir from the Creator of Multiple Intelligence Theory*.

After reading *A Synthesizing Mind* and watching several videos of Howard's talks, I had two questions for him. First, I wanted to know how he, a professor specializing in education, along with theories/studies of mind, could totally ignore the extensive damage that cultural Marxism (epitomized by the "woke mind virus") was wreaking in our universities. Shockingly, he didn't agree that it was causing such damage. Second, in his book, he describes himself as a "political junkie," but doesn't reveal his political beliefs. When I questioned him on this, he said he wanted to keep politics out of his work, but that he was a Democrat, and his favorite politician was Elizabeth Warren. Now, knowing that he was a Deep State-worshiping libtard, I invited him to attempt to deconstruct my chapter/article "Buddhist Politics 501." He declined, and I responded by asking him if he agreed with Elizabeth "Pocahontas" Warren's view that biological males should be allowed to compete in women's sports. Apparently offended by my reference to Warren as "Pocahontas" (an apropos nickname coined by Donald Trump in response to Warren's deceitful self-identification as an American Indian) and/or my audacity to intellectually (politically) challenge him (an esteemed Harvard professor), he permanently cut off communication with me.

In his 2017 book Trump and a Post-Truth World, *integral philosopher Ken Wilber writes, "And the only ones who should be allowed to work politically for a greater tomorrow—and who should indeed thus work—are those who truly understand that it is not necessary to do so…" Wilber, of course, doesn't identify who determines who should be allowed to work politically. Moreover, his entire book contradicts his statement that it is not necessary to do this work.*

If it weren't for Sam "Hare-Brained" Harris, Ken "Bald Ambition" Wilber would hold exclusive claim to the title "most overrated living philosopher." Wilber, an intellectual elitist, has, in effect, "privatized" the term "integral" (as it applies to an all-encompassing "theory of everything"). And his devoted followers contend that only his paradigm qualifies as true "integral theory." And, as implied from his statement you quoted, he seems to believe that he, and those who subscribe to his integral philosophy, should be the ones to determine who should be allowed to "work for a greater tomorrow."

In *Zen Mind, Thinker's Mind*, I devote a lengthy chapter to deconstructing the ideas for "integralizing" Buddhism that Wilber presents in his book *The Fourth Turning: Imagining the Evolution of an Integral Buddhism*. But my chapter only tangentially touches upon Wilber's disintegral sociopolitics. However, in *Electrical Christianity* (published in 2013), in the chapter "The Spiritual Politics of Jesus," I devote a subchapter—"The 'Four

Quadrants' of Integral Politics"—to considering Wilber's "integral" sociopolitical paradigm. What I want to do now (in light of the current toxic, uber-polarized political climate) is to reconsider what I wrote. Here [below] is the subchapter (with my reconsideration to follow).

The "Four Quadrants" of Integral Politics

Ken Wilber, the renowned integral philosopher, explains political systems and philosophies via a four-quadrant model and eight-level "Spiral Dynamics" hierarchy [Google for detailed descriptions]. According to Spiral Dynamics, the Ayn Rand and libertarian viewpoints you're espousing are only at level five of the eight-level political-evolutionary hierarchy. What's your response to this?

Ken Wilber is an avant-garde thinker worth reading and considering. However, although he unearths fertile new ground, he doesn't dig very deep into the soil; hence, his spiritual and political writings are less than profound and not truly "integral." I don't want to go off on an involved tangent, since many of you are unfamiliar with Wilber's writings and political philosophy, so I'll just briefly summarize my major criticisms of Wilber's Integral Politics for those of you interested in the subject.

First off, levels seven and eight of the Spiral Dynamics evolutionary political hierarchy that Wilber subscribes to are a complete joke—totally vague and nebulous New Age mumbo-jumbo. I won't waste my time or yours attempting to deconstruct this inchoate crap. Second, Wilber and Spiral Dynamics display their strong left-wing bias in level six. This level includes "postmodernism, egalitarianism, multiculturalism, subjective thinking, and decision-making through *consensus*." Postmodernism is utter drivel. The fact that Wilber gives any credence to this anti-philosophy is a black mark on his work. The placement of some of the other philosophies and/or orientations I've listed from level six bespeaks of a collectivist, or liberal-fascist, mindset. For example, "egalitarianism" and "multicultur- alism" exemplify reductionism rather than integralism, because instead of emphasizing equal individual rights and opportunity for all citizens, they focus attention on spe- cial-interest groups rather than on the *whole*—the organic "melting pot" that a truly free America would naturally be. Finally, the core description of level six— "Sacrifice self-interest now in order to gain acceptance and group harmony"—could be the mantra for any communist or fascist state. I'm sure Hitler's Nazi party would have merrily chanted it, because my late father, a German Jew who escaped from Germany in 1936, told me as much. In sum, it is farcical to place the various Spiral Dynamics "sixth-level" philosophies and orientations above Rand's "fifth-level" Objectivism.

I think you're being unfairly critical of Wilber, who is a very pos- itive New Age influence. He thinks globally and wants to bring about an integral world.

The international banking cartel, the Bilderberg group, and multinational corporations, like Monsanto, have beaten Wilber to the punch when it comes to creating an "integral" New World Order. While Wilber talks the talk, they walk the walk. I just hope he appreciates their Orwellian efforts when they tell him it's time for an "integral" computer chip to be implanted in his brain. The fact that Bill Clinton and Al Gore have displayed an interest in Wilber's writings tells me all I need to know regarding the relationship between the Globalists' and Wilber's "integral" politics. But again, I still think Wilber is worth reading. If you check my Spiritual Reading List, you'll see that he's on it.

How about Wilber's Four Quadrants?

Wilber's four-quadrant model—*Interior-Individual (Intentional), Exterior-Individual (Behavioral), Interior-Collective (Cultural), Exterior-Collective (Social)*—is a useful tool for understanding the individual-collective dialectic or interplay. But it isn't the ideal framework for understanding sociopolitical reality. The ideal framework for achieving this understanding is Ayn Rand's two pairs of poles: *individualism-statism* and *capitalism-socialism*. And these two pairs of poles, or four *isms*, provide us with the true "four quadrants" of sociopolitical reality. Let's now consider these poles and see how they apply to democratic and republican political systems.

If you believe in a *democratic* political system, the primacy of the government or a voting majority over the individual, then you are, by definition, a *statist*. By subscribing to this statist model of rule, you have, explicitly or implicitly, embraced a lynch-mob mentality, the fascist mindset that an individual is no more than a de facto slave, a government-owned human animal meant to be sacrificed to the dictates or decrees of the State or a voting majority. If, on the other hand, you believe in a *republican* political system, in inviolable, constitutionally guaranteed individual rights that the State cannot usurp, then you are an *individualist*. As such, your mentality is that of a sovereign man, an individual whose allegiance is to rationality and freedom rather than to a State that in any way seeks to limit or compromise human sovereignty.

Now let's move on to *capitalism-socialism*. True or laissez-faire capitalism, strictly speaking, is not an economic system; it is a social system based on the trader principle, wherein independent contractors freely exchange goods and services sans the interference of the Mafia State, the government. Socialism, by contrast, is a social system based on de facto State ownership and control of all goods and services. It is the Mafia model of government fully institutionalized, wherein Big "MoFoBro" owns the fruit of your labor and "gives" you whatever crumbs it wants. In return for your "service to the State," you receive "protection"—from everything but the tyrannical State itself.

You sound more dismissive of Wilber now than you did in Electrical Christianity. *What soured you on him?*

His devolution as a thinker, epitomized by his books *The Fourth Turning* and *Trump and a Post-Truth World*, both of which were published after *Electrical Christianity*. In *The Fourth Turning*, he reveals himself as a spiritual hack with no real understanding of Buddhism and what a fourth turning of its wheel should entail. And in *Trump and a Post-Truth World*, he displays gross sociopolitical ignorance and brainwashing. Like Sam Harris, Wilber suffers from acute TDS and has nothing but contempt for Trump supporters, whom, a la Hillary "Body Count" Clinton, he considers a basket of racist, sexist, xenophobic deplorables.

Donald Trump does not represent the Objectivist/right-libertarian ideals you advocate for. Why do you support him?

He's the best we Objectivist/libertarian right-wingers can realistically hope for at this time. My ideal candidate would be Rand Paul or Vivek Ramaswamy, but that's not happening. Hopefully, Trump learned from his mistakes (mainly bad personnel decisions and COVID blunders), and if elected in 2024, he will truly "drain the swamp" this time. The uniparty D.C. Swamp hates and fears him because he can't be bought or controlled by them. He not only threatens their multi-trillion-dollar racket of systematically ripping off the American people, but their very existence.

You argue that Wilber's four-quadrant model is inferior to (or less integral than) Ayn Rand's individualism-capitalism vs. statism-socialism dialectic for understanding sociopolitical reality. Can you elaborate further?

Unlike Wilber's model, Rand's dialectic provides the framework for understanding and explaining sociopolitical reality in any context, including the current zeitgeist. First, I'll employ Rand's dialectic to explain the fundamental dynamics that are now widening, and dramatically intensifying, the sociopolitical divide between the left and the right. Then, I'll apply it to explain where Wilber goes wrong in his *Trump and a Post-Truth World* thesis.

The (traditionally moderate) left, which used to be liberal in the semi-classical sense—supporting values such as equal rights, a color-blind meritocracy, free speech, legal-only immigration, and voter identification—has morphed into the (extremely radical) left, which not only champions the insane sociopolitical ideals and policies we've identified in our discourse, but also attempts to force them upon those of us (mainly on the right) who patently reject them.

Meanwhile, while the American left has moved dramatically further to the left, supporting authoritarian statism and socialism, a.k.a. Marxist-Fascism, the American (conservative) right (including the majority of Christians) has shifted further to the right and now embraces libertarian (or at least quasi-libertarian) ideals, which, thanks to the great Ron Paul, began to permeate the zeitgeist at the turn of the century. Thus, the divide now separating the left from the right has never been greater.

Do you see any chance for a unifying compromise, or at least a tolerable, sustainable coexistence, between the left and the right?

Not unless the left miraculously abandons its Marxist-Fascist agenda and excises its "woke mind virus." For, as Ayn Rand makes clear, in any compromise between good and evil, it is only evil that can benefit. Put bluntly, if the right loses this apocalyptic "Final Battle" against the left, you can kiss Western civilization and its Enlightenment values goodbye. The downward spiral of America will be so severe that red states will have no choice but to secede from the existing Union and form a new one.

Okay, back to Wilber. Where does he go wrong in his Trump and a Post-Truth World *thesis?*

Wilber blames level 6 (which, in the Spiral Dynamics hierarchy, correlates with the color green and the "progressive" left) for the left's failures and the resulting 2016 election of Donald Trump, whom he correlates with levels 5 (orange), 4 (blue), and 3 (red). In short, green, per Wilber, instead of building upon the good in orange with the positive ideals of level 6, self-destructed by not only jettisoning the necessary base of orange but also devolving into postmodern aperspectival madness, nihilism, and narcissism. While postmodern insanity has no doubt played a role in green's self-destruction, Wilber fails to acknowledge (and blame) classical and cultural Marxism as the major culprits in green's dystopian devolvement.

Anyone who watches James Lindsey's brilliant New Discourses YouTube videos will learn how cultural Marxism (really cultural Marxist-Fascism) emerged from classical Marxism and why it, not postmodernism, is the primary reason for the leftist lunacy that is now destroying the very fabric and ideals of Western civilization.

I could write a book deconstructing Wilber's integral idiocy (and I will gladly do so if someone offers me HUGE $$$ for the task). But at this point, rather than continue to rag on Wilber, I instead want to criticize Adi Da (1939-2008), a truly great spiritual master, who, sadly, was unable to apply his profound

spiritual realization/understanding to the subject of sociopolitics. He even wrote a book—*Not Two is Peace: The Ordinary
People's Way of Global Cooperative Order*—on the subject, which
ordinary people (the ignoranti) will vibe with, but which extraordinary people (the cognoscenti) won't. As a member of
the latter category, I saw fit, in 2012, to write a (since deleted
by Amazon) two-star review of the book, which I'll now present. (Note that the review was written before Klaus Schwab's
World Economic Forum [WEF] came into prominence, but
given Da's support for globalism and the U.N., it's likely that
he would have likewise backed the WEF agenda.)

NOT TWO IS PEACE (Adi Da)

Cooperation + Tolerance = Wrong Formula

I hate to be the fly in the ointment, the bearer of bad news,
but as *Not Two Is Peace* makes clear to me, the late Adi Da
Samraj (1939-2008) did not have the foggiest clue about
sociopolitics. Now before Daists and Da supporters jump
on me and impugn my motives for writing this review, I
want to make one thing clear: I am neither a disaffected
ex-devotee nor an angry Da basher. I am, in fact, a huge fan
of Adi Da's spiritual Dharma—I gave *The Knee of Listening*,
The Method of the Siddhas, and *Hridaya Rosary* five stars in
my Amazon reviews—and I freely admit that I wouldn't
have the comprehensive understanding of spirituality that
I do without having studied and practiced his teachings.
Moreover, anyone familiar with Da's teachings who reads
my spiritual writings will doubtless see Da's "stamp" on
them. In short, I love Da's spiritual Dharma but take umbrage with his political ideas.

I am an expert in sociopolitics. I majored in sociology at
the University of California, San Diego (1969-1973),
where I studied Marxism under the iconic neo-Marxist

professor Herbert Marcuse (author of the acclaimed text *One-Dimensional Man*). But years after graduating from college, I read Ayn Rand and Murray Rothbard, and these writings, along with my "real world" experiences, transformed me into a right-libertarian and a Ron Paul supporter when he ran for president. In short, over time, I morphed from a radical left-winger into what is now commonly referred to as a radical right-winger (really a "classical liberal").

Because this is a book review and not a book, I'll cut to the chase regarding Da's politics. In short, his formula for peace—Cooperation + Tolerance = Peace—is not always a formula for peace; but it is sometimes one for war, and there are examples throughout history that prove it. A notable one is the Munich Agreement struck between British Prime Minister Neville Chamberlain and Adolf Hitler. Chamberlain cooperated with Hitler, tolerating his limited territorial demands, but as history proved, Chamberlain's act of appeasement, his de facto implementation of the Cooperation + Tolerance = Peace formula, in the end cost the world millions of lives.

Ayn Rand's sagacious statement—"In any compromise between good and evil, it is only evil that can profit"—summarizes the flaw in Da's formula. It is great to cooperate with good, honest people, but do you really want to cooperate with evil, dishonest ones looking to do you or others harm? It's great, as an expression of freedom and liberty, to tolerate individual differences in sex, race, religion, personal appearance, etc., but do you want to tolerate any individual or government that seeks to limit your constitutionally guaranteed individual rights? I surely don't. In short, Da's formula for peace is not the right universal one, because it is only rationally applicable in certain, limited contexts; and in other contexts, exemplified by the Neville Chamberlain-Adolf Hitler fiasco, it fails miserably.

To my mind, the universal "formula" for peace that makes the most sense is the libertarian credo: "Do no harm." In other words, every individual is free to do as he or she pleases, so long as he or she doesn't interfere with anyone else's right to the same. As soon as an individual or government initiates force against a person or his property, then the libertarian credo is violated. According to this credo, statism (epitomized by government-en-FORCED anti-Constitutional negation of individual rights and acts of theft via fascistic, neo-Marxist policies) is explicitly rejected. And when this anti-freedom, anti-liberty statism escalates into New World Order Globalism, then the entire world becomes, in the words of Alex Jones, a "Prison Planet." And the "Warden" running the "Prison" is none other than the International Banking Cartel and the lackey "world leaders" (politicians) doing its bidding.

According to Rand, the sociopolitical poles are clear: statism/socialism vs. individualism/capitalism. I'm firmly in the camp of the latter, but because this is just a review and not a sociopolitical treatise, I'll refer you to some sources that expound upon my choice and might make you question Da's formula: Watch Stefan Molyneux's video "The Story of Your Enslavement"; Google and read the essay "The Anatomy of the State" by Murray Rothbard; get the books *The Creature from Jekyll Island: A Second Look at the Federal Reserve* by G. Edward Griffin and *The True Story of the Bilderberg Group* by Daniel Estulin; and read my chapter on politics in my forthcoming text *Electrical Christianity* (available Spring 2013).

I read Not Two Is Peace, *and it's hard to believe that Da ignorantly supported globalism, the U.N., and the blatantly defective formula "cooperation + tolerance = peace." What's even harder to believe is that, with your review expunged by Amazon, the dozens of remaining reviews are all positive. How stupid can spiritual people be?*

So stupid that most every prominent spiritual guru/teacher is a sociopolitical ignoramus, a sucker for leftist ideals. For example, Osho (Rajneesh) was an unabashed supporter of Marxism, as is the Dalai Lama, who is too brainless to comprehend that Marxist China is responsible for the demise of Tibet. I recently watched Eckhart Tolle being interviewed by Russell Brand (on his uber-popular, politically oriented YouTube channel), and, unsurprisingly, the foggy Tolle displayed utter sociopolitical ignorance, while the clueless subscribers to Brand's channel left comments congratulating him for what were no more than vague, nebulous, and trite New Age platitudes. And, of course, there is New Age "spiritual guru" Marianne Williams, a socialist "bubble brain" who is running for president in 2024. Williams is not only a spiritual joke (big into the balderdash-infested *A Course in Miracles*), but also a political one, supporting neo-Marxist policies (such as reparations and student loan forgiveness) that tax-paying citizens should not have to subsidize.

You haven't mentioned Sadhguru, perhaps the most popular guru in the world at this time. He hangs out with the global elites at the World Economic Forum.

Yep, Sadhguru (Jaggi Vasudev), who is not a Sat Guru, but a pop guru, a la Eckhart Tolle, is yet another politically ignorant spiritual leader. He advocated for the deadly COVID-19 vaccines, buys into the climate-change scam, and, of course, supports the evil, tyrannical World Economic Forum (WEF). If you want to know what ideologically drives WEF founder and economic chairman Klaus Schwab, notice that in some of his interviews, a bust of Vladimir Lenin is prominently displayed on the shelf behind his desk. In other words, he is really a Marxist, but because he knows that "Marxism" is a dirty word, he "creatively" rebranded it as "stakeholder capitalism."

[Note: The 86-year-old Schwab retired from his post as economic chairman of the WEF in May of 2024, several months after our WEF consideration. But the WEF, sans Schwab at the helm, will continue to foist its evil globalist agenda upon the world.]

Many months ago (before Schwab retired), I wrote a review of the WEF book/manifesto *Covid-19: The Great Reset* by Klaus Schwab and Thierry Malleret. This review makes clear my view on Schwab and the WEF.

COVID-19: THE GREAT RESET (Klaus Schwab and Thierry Malleret)

The Totalitarian Marxist-Fascist Reset

This book was exactly what I expected from a couple of dictatorial, dumbfuck Marxist-Fascist professors pushing a New World Order (NWO) sociopolitical agenda. Not only are these two professors philosophically retarded (as are all left-wing "thinkers"), they are also hubris-bloated and allergic to facts. If the globalist agenda they argue for weren't so evil and dystopian, it would almost be laughable, because only ivory-tower idiots like these two academic clowns could imagine the Slave New World they do.

Schwab and Malleret write:

"Without delay we need to set in motion the Great Reset. This is not a 'nice-to-have' but an absolute necessity. Failing to address and fix the deep-rooted ills of our societies and economies could heighten the risk that, as throughout history, ultimately a reset will be imposed by violent shocks like conflicts and even revolutions. It is incumbent upon us to take the bull by the horns. The pandemic gives us this chance: it represents a rare but narrow window of opportunity to reflect, reimagine and reset our world."

If Schwab and Malleret were honest, they would have instead written: The PLANdemic gives us this chance: it represents a rare but narrow window of opportunity (FOR US) to TO-TALISTICALLY and FASCISTICALLY reset OUR world.

What's especially laughable is the authors' (of course disingenuous) account of the genesis of COVID-19:

"By now, an increasing number of scientists have shown that it is in fact the destruction of biodiversity caused by humans that is the source of new viruses like COVID-19. These researchers have coalesced around the new discipline of 'planetary health' that studies the subtle and complex connections that exist between the well-being of humans, other living species and entire ecosystems, and their findings have made it clear that the destruction of biodiversity will increase the number of pandemics."

We now know that COVID-19 is a bio-weapon engineered in the Wuhan lab through nefarious gain-of-function research. And it's more than likely that the Coronavirus didn't escape from the Wuhan lab but was intentionally released to wreak MURDEROUS global havoc upon the world, thereby facilitating the Great Reset. If you are naive enough to believe that the authors didn't/don't know this, that they buy their own bullshit story of the destruction of biodiversity as the source of COVID-19, then I've got some oceanfront property in Nevada to sell you.

The authors write:

"Many of us are pondering when things will return to normal. The short response is: never. Nothing will ever return to the 'broken' sense of normalcy that prevailed prior to the crisis because the coronavirus pandemic marks a fundamental inflection point in our global trajectory… COVID 19 has dramatically torn up the existing script of how to govern countries and live with others and take part in the global economy."

What is the essence of this "new script" on how to govern? Per the authors, it's "the return of 'big' government." They write:

"Looking to the future, governments will most likely, but with different degrees of intensity, decide that it's in the best interest of society to rewrite some of the rules of the game and permanently increase their role… How will this expanded role of governments manifest itself? A significant element of new 'bigger' government is already in place with the vastly increased and quasi-immediate government control of the economy."

In short, the authors want to "redefine the terms of our social contract" through global governance. They write:

"The more nationalism and isolationism pervade the global polity, the greater the chance that global governance loses its relevance and becomes ineffective. Sadly, we are now at this critical juncture. Put bluntly, we live in a world in which nobody is really in charge…Without appropriate global governance, we will become paralyzed in our attempts to address and respond to global challenges."

Those of us "in the know" know what this global governance really means—a dictatorial Ruling Elite not subject to their own dictates that will sociopolitically/economically control the entire world. The authors have nothing to say about individual rights (including property rights) in their envisaged New World Order, because in their Slave New World there will be none. As Schwab puts it, "You will own nothing and be happy," while, of course, the Ruling Elite, multi-billion-aires, will be above and exempt from the draconian Marxist-Fascist laws they will impose on the subjugated masses.

Those "in the know" know that the globalist left conspired with the Deep State left in the U.S. to make sure that Donald Trump, who champions the MAGA nationalism the authoritarian globalists oppose, lost the 2020 presidential election. The globalist left's foisting of the COVID pandemic upon the world not only undermined Trump's booming economy but also enabled widespread fraudulent mail-in voting, effectively rigging the election for Joe Biden. If these New World Order tyrants ever gain control of the globe, honest elections will be a thing of the past.

If you have any doubt about the authors' allegiance to tyrannical China, consider their absurd statement, "Unlike the Soviet Union, China is not seeking to impose their ideology around the world." Only Matrix-bound idiots believe this. And regarding the adversarial relations between the U.S. (under Trump) and China, they opine: "There isn't a right view as to which country is wrong or right." Only a totalitarian Marxist-Fascist would not view China as wrong, as evil, as an enemy of free speech, free religion, free markets, and individual rights. Only a Marxist-Fascist would support their tyrannical takeover of Hong Kong and planned invasion of Taiwan.

The authors assert that "the world needs the WHO [World Health Organization] now more than ever." What a joke. The uber-corrupt, "China-centric" WHO (doubtless in bed with the WEF) failed in its role as a global watch dog that could have stopped, or greatly curtailed, the initial spread of COVID-19 out of China. The WHO also failed to immediately force an investigation of the Wuhan lab, protecting China from other countries learning the truth about the origins of COVID-19. And Donald Trump, in response, appropriately, froze U.S. funding of the WHO.

Being the nefarious, allergic-to-facts Marxist-Fascist libtards that they are, the authors push bullshit lies and narratives to buttress their argument for the Great Reset. For example, they argue that the Great Reset will create a better world that is "more inclusive and equitable."

The so-called "free world" does not exclude anyone, but the Marxist-Fascism that the Great Reset embraces is all about excluding (and censoring/canceling) those who do not embrace the WEF's agenda (which, predictably, has NOTHING to say about free speech and an end to Big Tech censorship and cancel culture). The "progressive" Great Reset left eschews the term "equality" (of opportunity) and instead pushes the term "equity," which grants the Ruling Elite carte blanche to dictatorially determine socioeconomic outcomes, meaning the right to arbitrarily steal and redistribute money and property.

The authors, like all lamebrained leftists, love throwing around vague platitudinous terms that they fail to provide evidence for. For example, they argue for systemic "fairness," citing systemic racism in America as unfairness. There is no systemic racism (against blacks or Hispanics) in America. Right-wing political pundits Ben Shapiro and Larry Elder have invited their detractors to point out specific examples of said racism in America, and no one has been able to do so.

Regarding "shocking" systemic racism in America, the authors also mention Black Lives Matter (BLM). But, of course, they fail to mention that BLM are trained Marxists whose social agenda is to end the police and the nuclear family. Moreover, the by far major reason for the black social plight is the destruction of the black nuclear family, caused by long-standing left-wing welfare policies. Unsurprisingly, the authors have nothing to say about this, just as they have nothing to say about the fact that 97% of blacks are murdered by other blacks, and that the vast majority of these epidemic-level murders take place in cities controlled by the authors' fellow leftists.

The authors include a chapter, "Environmental Reset," in their book, which reveals them as either stupid or willing to lie to push the narrative of a climate-change crisis intertwined with the pandemic as justification for the "Great Reset." In this chapter, the authors not only consider COVID-19 as a product of climate change but also link air pollution with it. If the authors had an iota of integrity, they'd not only consider the counter-arguments that debunk the theory of a current climate-change crisis, but also identify the chief benefits of global warming.

The authors, in their arguments for global governance, emphasize the need for cooperation. Unbeknownst to these cognitively challenged authors, everything is contextual, including cooperation. As Ayn Rand makes clear, when good cooperates with evil, only good evil can benefit. In other words, my libertarian brethren and I have ZERO interest in cooperating with the authors and their uber-evil NWO Marxist-FASCIST brotherhood.

Wow! You don't mince words. So, from what you're saying, the pole of socialism/statism can be expanded to socialism/statism/globalism because globalism, meaning global governance by a ruling elite, amounts to statism on a global scale, which, of course, can conspire with statism on a national scale to totally enslave given populations.

Bravo! You nailed it. And, of course, that is what we see happening now, as Klaus Schwab, George Soros, and others of their ilk seek to impose their globalist agenda on nations, some of which are more than willing to work with them. A prime example of a compliant national co-partner is Canada under Prime Minister Justin Trudeau. Canada is now so far gone as a free-speech nation that, as we speak, it is (through the arm of the Ontario College of Psychologists) forcing renowned psychologist Dr. Jordan Peterson to undergo a "re-education" program (or have his clinical license revoked) simply because his sane anti-Wokeism views are antithetical to their insane pro-Wokeism ones.

You've pretty thoroughly riffed on the current sociopolitical milieu, making it clear how dire and disturbing the situation is. Do you have anything more to add on this?

Not unless I wanted to delve deeply into specifics and turn our discussion into a protracted marathon. And because our present discussion is meant to comprise a chapter in *Nonduality and Mind Only*, and not a book, it suffices as an overview of the current sociopolitical confrontation, or "Final Battle," as political pundit David Horowitz describes it. Hence, I'll now conclude by briefly applying Hegelian dialectic to analyze the current left (socialism/statism) vs. right (capitalism/individualism) battle.

From my perspective, at the current juncture in the "late-time epoch" (Adi Da's term) in which we are now living, the World Spirit has "moved" to bring the left/right opposition to a head. Thanks to the Internet, social media, and the Donald Trump phenomenon, a monumental mass of people have become sociopolitically "red-pilled." These newly awakened masses (on top of those who were already awake) now understand that the establishment Democrat and Republican parties are two sides of the same uber-corrupt, uber-authoritarian anti-constitutional coin and, as such, form a malevolent uniparty. The hardline Marxist-Fascist Democrats have captured the federal institutions and agencies, while the mainstream Republican Party members, comprised of RINOs (Republicans in name only), are more than happy to get fat and rich playing their role as faux opposition. But when big-name RINOs—George Bush, Mitt Romney, Dick and

Liz Cheney, et al. —refused to support (and even condemned) a true Republican President, Donald Trump (who can't be bought or controlled by the Deep State D.C. uniparty), that awakened millions of previously "asleep" people to political reality. And when, in 2023, the Deep State launched multiple bogus lawsuits to prevent Trump from regaining the presidency in 2024, then followed it up with anti-democratic attempts to remove him from states' primary ballots, even more asleep people morphed into awakened patriots.

If Trump hadn't won in 2016 and appointed three Republican Supreme Court justices, and the Republican Party hadn't (barely) won a House majority in 2022, America as a Constitutional Republic would be all but over.

You've got that right. Elections would have become federally controlled, and the demonic Democrat Party would then have had carte blanche to rig elections and comprehensively institute their "progressive" uniparty Marxist-Fascist agenda.

So what happens now?

It's early 2024 as we now contemplate the possibilities regarding America. Will the 2024 election be the "final pronouncement," bringing the left/right battle to a concluding head? No way. It will provide us with many answers, but with the poles of the political dialectic firmly encamped in diametrical opposition to each other, there can be no synthesis to this thesis (right-wing constitutional republican) vs. antithesis (left-wing mob-rule democratic) dialectic without a revolution of sorts, because neither side is willing to capitulate to the other.

If there is to be a synthesis, it has to be with the right politically victorious; for if the left triumphs, there can be no synthesis, only an America as a Marxist-Fascist banana republic. As I made clear in my article "Buddhist Politics 501," the right-wing pole of constitutional republicanism allows for the left-wing pole of collectivism—in privatized forms—but when the State displaces the primacy of constitutional republicanism, supplanting it with socialist statism, it is not possible for the pole of individualism / capitalism to function freely, outside the tentacles of the predatory State.

The majority of people reading our exchange won't have the background knowledge and / or information to fully digest the content of our discussion. What resource recommendations do you have for them?

I now recommend three books for those new to sociopolitical awakening: *The Revolution: A Manifesto* by Ron Paul, *The Ayn Rand Lexicon: Objectivism from A to Z*, and *The Creature from Jekyll Island: A Second Look at the Federal Reserve* by G. Edward Griffin. Some YouTube channels worth checking out (in no particular order) include: Victor Davis Hanson, Michael Savage, Dinesh D'Souza, Facts Matter with Roman Balmakov, New Discourses (James Lindsay), The Dave Rubin Show, Valuetainment, Megyn Kelly, Dave Smith, Styxhexenhammer666, Tom Woods TV, John Stossel, Mark Dice, Liberal Hivemind, Viva Frei, Nick Freitas, Timcast IRL, Vivek Ramaswamy, Thomas Sowell, Ben Shapiro, Alan Dershowitz, Benny Johnson, Official ACLJ, Judicial Watch, Wolves And Finance, The Epoch Times, The Mark Levin Show, Newsmax, Tucker Carlson, Doug in Exile, and The Clay Travis & Buck Sexton Show (also available as the daily radio show that replaced The Rush Limbaugh Show).

Final question: How do you relate the dialectical sociopolitical wheel to nonduality and Mind-Only?

The nondual One Mind, *Siva*, created a world of duality and polar opposites for His fun and entertainment. As Hegel makes clear, dialectical opposites fuel evolutionary struggle and growth; so it was predictable that the two "extreme" sociopolitical poles—left-wing

Marxist-Fascism and right-wing libertarianism/conservatism—would eventually square off. And now, this battle royale is seemingly coming to a head—and the result will either be a synthesis (with libertarianism/conservatism trumping Marxist-Fascism), or a painful, and perhaps violent, separation between the two sides. From the Divine's perspective, it's all theater; but for us humans enmeshed in *Maya*, it's a serious, even apocalyptic, matter.

When it's understood that this world of duality and polar opposites arises within Mind, or *Siva*, as a modification of Him, then the nondual perspective that there is only the One Mind is maintained. But from our limited perspective as separate, distinct beings in a phenomenal universe, wherein existence has primacy over consciousness, the duality and polar opposites seem all too real.

So are they real?

Of course, because nothing unreal can come from, or arise within, the Real (meaning Mind). Whatever exists is real, but from our human perspective, the ontological status of existents must be differentiated. And most importantly, if we are to attain Enlightenment, we must differentiate between created phenomenal reality (*Maya*) and uncreated Ultimate Reality (Mind).

What's next in our ongoing discussions?

We've tackled the dialectical sociopolitical wheel. Next on our agenda is the dialectical sociocultural wheel, the final piece to my new Tree of Life.

CHAPTER TWELVE

Beyond *The Phenomenology of Spirit,* Part 3

The Horizontal Axis of the Dialectical Sociocultural Wheel

Okay, you've got the dialectical sociocultural wheel across from the dialectical sociopolitical wheel in your 3-Dimensional Tree of Life [Diagram3]. What can you say about it?

Broadly speaking, whereas politics pertains to the policies (or laws) in a given geographical area, culture refers to the values, customs, and norms cultivated in that area. It is commonly said that culture is upstream from politics, meaning that the laws in a given geographical area generally reflect the prevalent cultural milieu. Since both politics and culture are inextricably social and societal in nature, this provides us with the terms "sociopolitical" and "sociocultural."

The two poles of the dialectical sociocultural wheel—self-identity/self-expression versus relationships/partnerships on the horizontal axis and home/family versus livelihood/life mission on the vertical axis—represent the four cardinal departments of social and societal life, which correspond with the four cardinal houses (first, fourth, seventh, tenth) in astrology [see Diagram 5]. In fact, some might argue that the two poles of the dialectical sociopolitical wheel, when "creatively" considered, also correspond with the four cardinal houses.

Livelihood/Life Mission

Relationships/Partnerships

Self-identity/Self-expression

Home/Family

Career, long-term goals, structure, status, reputation, public image, masculinity, men, fathers, experts, fame.

Groups, friends, social awareness, humanitarianism, technology, hopes and wishes, the future.

Travel, wisdom, philosophy, higher education, law & religion, cross-cultural relations, learning, ethics.

Merging, sex, intimacy, shared finances, inheritances, taxes, loans, assets, property, joint ventures, goals, mystery, partner's resources.

Endings, healing, closure, spirituality, solitude, karma, old age, afterlife, what's hidden, limiting beliefs, subconscious.

Relationships, marriage, contracts, business partners, equality, sharing, interpersonal style.

Self, appearances, beginnings, the body, first impressions, attitude, identity, approach to life.

Health, fitness, systems, analytical nature, pets, work habits, organization, sense of usefulness, service given.

Money, work, income, daily routines, values, material possessions, priorities, habits, your job and work ethic.

The mind/ thinking, communication, siblings, social activity/interests, neighbours, early education.

Home, roots, family, self-care, emotions, foundations, mother, children, women, femininity.

Romance, love, affairs, play, creativity, fertility, childlike spirit, joy, self-expression, drama.

10 9 8 7 6 5 4 3 2 1 11 12

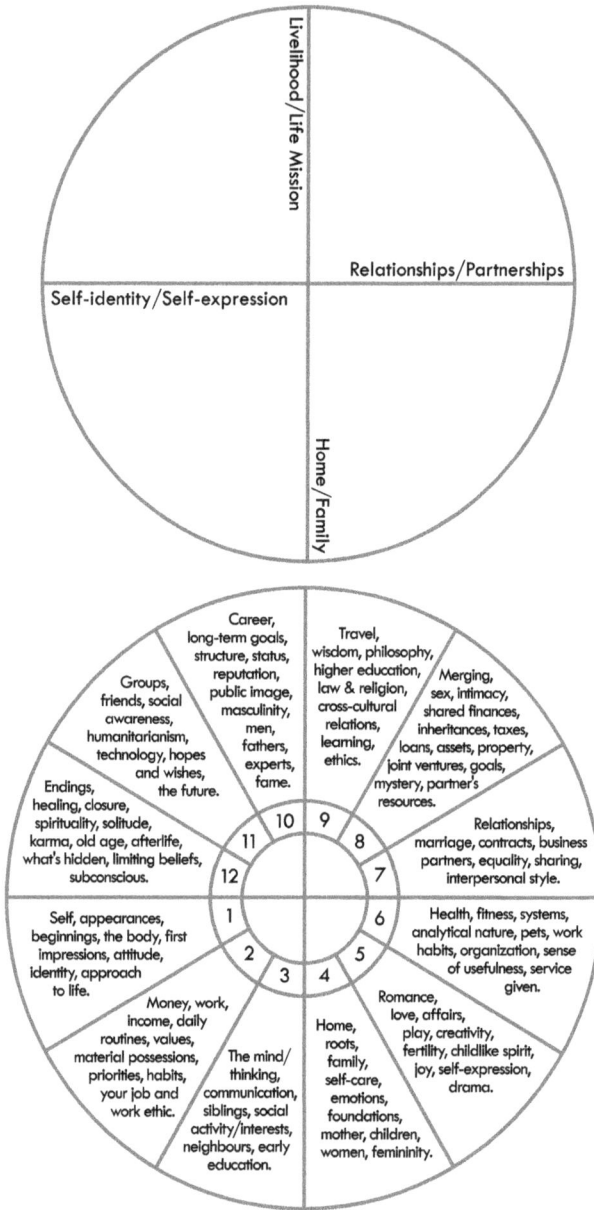

Diagram 5. The Dialectical Sociocultural Wheel and Cardinal Astrological Houses

The extreme polarization we now see sociopolitically also exists socioculturally, which is not surprising, given that culture precedes (and shapes) politics. On the horizontal axis, traditional male and female self-identity/self-expression is being subverted/perverted by the "woke" left, which champions "gender fluidity," the absurd (and socially/societally destructive) idea that one's imaginary (or even surgically influenced) self-identity trumps intractable biological reality. Moreover, this self-identity subversion/perversion extends into self-expression, epitomized by biological males who, pretending to be females, compete in, and dominate, women's sports, making a mockery of them.

The destructive ramifications of the breakdown of clear-cut male/female distinctions go beyond sports.

For sure. But since we're only briefly considering socioculture in the context of Kabbalah and Mind-Only nondualism, our discussion on the subject will necessarily be limited. Those interested in the subject can find an abundance of additional material online and elsewhere.

Moving on to relationships/partnerships in our consideration, what stands out is the impact that the breakdown of traditional, biologically-based self-identities has on relationships—including legal partnerships, especially marriages. Same-sex marriages are now common, and we even see same-sex couples with children. My POV is that marriage contracts between consenting adults should be a private matter; so while I consider same-sex marriages (and homosexuality and trans-sexuality) a perversion, I support the right of adults to legally "marry" (or contractually partner with) any consenting other. That said, I staunchly oppose censorship/cancel culture that prohibits those such as myself from calling a spade a spade, meaning identifying perversion as perversion.

Why are such relations perversions? Because they can't produce life, only disease. For example, when a man sticks his penis into another man's anus, an orifice biologically intended solely for defecation, that is the primary means by which AIDS is transmitted.

It seems like the Democrat left is all about identity politics.

Identity politics is cultural Marxism in action. Because the Democrats can't gain dictatorial control of America through classical Marxism (meaning anti-capitalist socioeconomic class warfare), they resort to cultural Marxism (meaning race/gender warfare) as the means to their end. Cultural Marxism (a.k.a. Wokeism) provides the vehicle for the left to censor/cancel those on the right. Through censorship/cancel culture, they effectively monopolize mainstream media and the educational system, brainwashing the masses to embrace their narratives, which demonize those on the right, portraying them as racist, sexist bigots and threats to democracy.

Per Wikipedia: "The term 'Cultural Marxism' refers to a far-right antisemitic conspiracy theory which misrepresents the Frankfurt School as being responsible for modern progressive movements, identity politics, and political correctness. The conspiracy theory posits that there is an ongoing and intentional academic and intellectual effort to subvert Western society via a planned culture war that undermines the Christian values of traditionalist conservatism and seeks to replace them with culturally liberal values." What can you say about this?

Wikipedia has been captured by leftists who can't compete in the arena of ideas, so they resort to labeling anyone who disputes mainstream (including Marxist-Fascist) ideas as a "conspiracy theorist." I'm Jewish, and so are some of my friends, and we *know* that cultural Marxism is a reality, not an antisemitic conspiracy theory. I studied Marxism, including "cultural Marxism" (though we didn't use that term for it), directly under its "father," Herbert Marcuse, the foremost representative of the Frankfurt School. And at meetings with fellow Marxist students of Marcuse, we would discuss Mao Zedong's "Cultural Revolution" in China, and ways to add a "U.S.-flavored" cultural dimension to classical Marxism, because we realized that classical Marxism, in and of itself, could not consummate a Communist revolution in America.

My suggestion to those who doubt the reality of cultural Marxism, or who want deeper, more detailed information on the subject, is to watch any, or all, of the following YouTube videos: "Mao in America" (Dinesh D'Souza), "American Maoism," "Maoism with American Characteristics," and "Woke, Mao, and the American Cultural Revolution" (New Discourses). And for those who want the lowdown on Wikipedia, check out the YouTube videos "The Internet's Largest Source of Misinformation" and "It All Makes Sense Now" (Mark Dice).

It seems like social media is the final battleground, the principal medium where we on the right can fight back against the left and its Marxist agenda.

Very true. The left is doing everything in their power to shut the door on free speech on the Internet. Thankfully, Elon Musk bought Twitter (now X), rescuing it from near-total FBI (Federal Bureau of Injustice) control. And praise to Rumble for resisting mass pressure from the leftist establishment to cancel/censor prominent voices (with Russell Brand [in September, 2023] being the latest) who dare to question/expose mainstream narratives and propaganda.

Okay, what synthesis do you see emerging from the current self-identity/self-expression pole and its relationships/partnerships antipole?

The leftist (or cultural Marxist) idea of self-identity/self-expression is not just hyper-focused on race and gender; it is also tied to social action (or expression) pertaining to racial and gender identity. And this translates into the leftist push for Affirmative Action and DEI (Diversity, Equity, Inclusion). Hence, leftist social action transforms these "pseudo-individuals" into hivemind "social justice warriors" who resort to censorship/cancel culture to fascistically force their "woke" agenda upon those of us who reject it.

The leftist ideal of sociocultural relationships/partnerships places them under the umbrella of the State. Like Hillary Clinton, her fellow hard leftists believe that it "takes a village" to raise your kids, to inculcate them with the "right ideas" about race, gender, and the State. The more extreme leftists, epitomized by Black Lives Matter (BLM), believe in the dissolution of traditional marriage and the nuclear family, so that the Marxist State can totally dictate "right social action," enforced by social credit scores that punish anyone with the gall to question the State's agenda.

How about the left's war on men?

The left has all but cut off men's balls, depicting "real men" as suffering from "toxic masculinity." It's no coincidence that male testosterone levels have dropped to record lows, as "progressive" leftist ideology has gained ascendancy over the past few decades. Leftist ideology is all about hivemind subservience to the dictates of the domineering State. And for the left to achieve the totalitarian dominance it seeks, it must emasculate "real men," who typically gravitate to anti-statist libertarian sociopolitics. Thus, the ideal man, per "woke" leftists, is the latte-sipping "soy boy" who believes that men can menstruate and get pregnant.

Donald Trump is an "old school" real man with BIG balls; so he's a BIG threat to the left, which cannot "tame" and control him. His antipode, and the prototypical leftist man, is current Attorney General Merrick Garland, a pathetic spineless cuck who sold his manhood and soul to the left. Just as W.C. Fields never met a drink he didn't like, the wimpy Garland, now overseer of the corrupt U.S. banana republic justice system, never met a lie he didn't like.

Although we see charismatic "front men," such as Barack Obama, and now Gavin Newsom, who seem to belie my description of the stereotypical male Democrat politician, it's just a show, because in reality, they're just actors, fake real men who, unlike Donald Trump, are scripted purveyors of Deep State propaganda, narratives, and lies. In fact, prior to becoming Barack Obama, Barry Soetoro was known as "Bathhouse Barry," a closet gay man who loved to "take it up the old wazoo." Moreover, per the late Joan Rivers (research her untimely death) and many others, Barack's "wife," Michelle, is really his "husband," Michael.

When the mainstream left seeks to destroy a man who does not conform to their ideology and/or dictates, they, when possible, dredge up female accusers of rape and/or sexual assault from the man's distant past. These women, who never saw fit to file charges against the man before, now suddenly, decades later, decide to do so. Although these accusations and charges seldom amount to anything substantive, they sully the man's reputation and can destroy his life. Supreme Court Justice Brett Kavanaugh, actor/political pundit Russell Brand, and Donald Trump are three prominent victims of this ploy.

It now seems common for women to accuse rich and famous men of rape and/or sexual assault.

It's open season for gold diggers, because even if their accusations
are proven false (as they often are), they rarely face legal consequences for them, which is crazy, indicative of how anti-male
the justice system is. One of the most egregious recent cases of
this involves MLB pitching star Trevor Bauer, who was falsely
accused of sexual assault (and never charged with a crime). Yet,
simply on the basis of the unproven allegation, MLB suspended
him from the league for two years. Unfortunately, the leftist ral-
lying cry "believe all women" has become the pervading social
norm, and men, all too often, are victims of this madness.

*Okay, so how do we dialectically resolve this social/societal devolve-
ment of interpersonal relationships?*

Through a cultural "revolution" (which amounts to a cultural
reversion to the "good old days," when men were "real men"
and women were "real women"). "Wokeism" (meaning cultural
Marxism) needs to be eradicated socially and societally. It causes
depolarization, confusion, and warfare between the (only two)
sexes. Polarization (meaning maximal masculinity for men, maximal femininity for women) eliminates confusion between the
sexes; and with male/female roles made clear, inter-sex warfare
is dramatically reduced, as men no longer seek to be (or be like)
women, and women no longer seek to be (or be like) men.

Therefore, the thesis (masculinity) and its antithesis (femininity)
are no longer blurred and confused, but clearly delineated and
emphasized. And the end result, or synthesis, is a healthy, natural
"play" between the sexes, rather than the current acrimonious
one that demonizes men for so-called "toxic masculinity" and
punishes them before they are found guilty of a real crime.

Finally, in contrast to the "woke" social justice warriors who,
fascistically, seek to dictate what sexual roles are acceptable—
and even worse, to censor/cancel those who oppose their

dictates—the synthesis I envision not only allows for roles (between consenting adults) that are contrary to the "polarized norms" I advocate for, but most importantly, for the free speech that allows people to openly criticize behavior they find objectionable.

In other words, your vision, or synthesis, allows for what you consider to be sexual perversion (by, and between, consenting adults), but for the right of people, such as yourself, to freely, publicly identify this behavior as perversion, rather than as an alternative form of "normal and healthy."

That's right. In short, it's simply about calling a spade a spade, and the right to do so—two things the Marxist-FASCIST left opposes.

Anything more you want to add to our discussion on the horizontal dialectical sociocultural axis of self and others, as it pertains to the current zeitgeist?

We could continue sine die on the subject of interpersonal relations, partnerships, and roles in the context of the current zeitgeist, but because our focus is much broader than that, we need to move on and leave that consideration to others. Instead, I'll conclude our discussion by presenting a Hindu tantric perspective on the subject.

From the perspective of Hindu tantrism, Ultimate (unmanifest) Reality is *Siva-Shakti* (Male-Female). IOW, it is explicitly two, and only two, genders. And from this perspective, (manifest) reality, which derives from and reflects (unmanifest) Reality, is also a two-gender affair. Hence, instead of saying Reality/reality is "turtles all the way down," we could (and should) say it is "*Siva-Shakti* all the way down."

CHAPTER THIRTEEN

Beyond *The Phenomenology of Spirit,* Part 4

The Vertical Axis of the Dialectical Sociocultural Wheel

The vertical axis of my dialectical sociocultural wheel has home/family opposite livelihood/life mission. The Marxist-Fascist left is not content with just undoing the traditional horizontal axis of self-identity/self-expression opposite relationships/partnerships; it is also intent on taking apart the traditional vertical axis.

The Marxist-Fascist left (which is now synonymous with the Democrat Party) is all about expanding the power and control of the government—the State—and to accomplish this, it must lay siege to the nuclear family unit. When Hillary "Hell's Belle" Clinton says it takes a village to raise your child, she means that the State is the de facto parent, not you. Black Lives Matter (BLM), a self-avowed Marxist organization (which the mainstream left has praised and supported), openly declares their aversion to the traditional family unit: "We disrupt the Western-prescribed nuclear family structure requirement by supporting each other as extended families and 'villages' that collectively care for one another."

What is the effect of dismantling the nuclear family? The following excerpt from the Heritage Foundation's website (heritage.org) provides an example:

In a February 2020 article in the *Atlantic,* University of Virginia professor Brad Wilcox and Brigham Young University associate professor Hal Boyd note: "One federal report found that children living in a household with an unrelated adult were about nine times more likely to be physically, sexually, or emotionally abused than children raised in an intact nuclear family." That hardly makes the case for undoing family and outsourcing familial duties to a collective of strangers.

Public schools are now notorious for attempting to wrest educational control of students from parents.

Yes, it's about indoctrinating rather than educating children. The goal is to turn them into good little statists, with the same perverted values as their teachers, most of whom are Democrats.

Destruction of the nuclear family is not enough for the radical left. They also want to wrest home ownership from us.

World Economic Forum (WEF) founder and chairman Klaus Schwab, the NWO globalist kingpin [until he retired in May 2024], summarizes the radical left's view of home ownership with his infamous mantra: "You will own nothing and be happy." In other words, Schwab and his cronies' idea of "economic freedom" is their freedom to own everything, while you own nothing.

It's no coincidence that giant multinational corporations associated with the WEF are currently buying up a higher-than-ever percentage of single-family homes in America. For example, Blackstone, the world's largest private investment firm (with a trillion dollars under management) and an ally of the WEF, now specializes in buying single-family homes that banks have foreclosed on.

On the upper pole of the sociocultural vertical axis, livelihood and life mission have also been subverted/perverted by the left.

What hasn't been subverted/perverted by the left? The left is all about dictatorial control of virtually every aspect of human life. Their God is the State, Big Brother; and in the depraved eyes of these statists, individual rights are to be subordinated to the dictates of Big Brother, which, subversively—through rigged elections, censorship, cancel culture, brainwashing in public schools and universities, collusion with corporate America, a corrupt legal system, and a controlled mainstream media—seeks to establish a Marxist-Fascist state, nationally and globally.

If your livelihood or life mission (including religious or political work) doesn't cohere with the Marxist-Fascist ideals of the statists, you run the risk of being cancelled and/or persecuted. The most glaring example of this right now [October 2023] is the Deep State's ongoing witch hunt against Donald Trump, which is aimed at preventing him from regaining the presidency in 2024. Those prominently associated with Trump and his MAGA movement are also targets of these banana republic tyrants, who have "weaponized" government agencies (national, state, and city) as "attack dogs" to go after them.

I just learned that the ACLJ (American Center for Law and Justice) has uncovered (through FOIA requests) massive targeting of Christians by the IRS.

That's not at all surprising. Under Barack Obama's presidency, the IRS targeted Tea Party organizations, but, of course, no one was imprisoned for this crime. In other words, if you're on the Deep State's team, you're virtually immune from legal prosecution (even if your crimes are as egregious as Hillary Clinton's and Joe Biden's), but if you're a patriot into championing anti-statist ideals of constitutional republicanism, you'll

be mercilessly prosecuted for virtual nothing burgers (as exemplified by the inhumane treatment and draconian sentences
inflicted upon by those who, sans weapons, merely occupied
the Capitol building on January 6).

*On the cultural front, DEI [Diversity, Equity, Inclusion] now strongly
influences hiring practices and promotions; in other words, livelihood.*

You've got that right. Instead of advocating for a color-blind
meritocracy (which is anti-racist and anti-sexist), the "progressive" (really progressively more Marxist-Fascist) left loves to
discriminate against those it deems their "oppressors," usually
meaning white males, whom they believe are disproportion-
ately successful only because of their "white privilege."

The end result is the promotion or appointment of incompe-
tent people (usually social justice warriors), who look to over-
ride the U.S. Constitution (and destroy the republic) through
the implementation of their racist and/or sexist Marxist-
Fascist ideals and policies.

*Typical examples of this include Vice President Kamala Harris (who
can hardly utter a single coherent sentence) and Supreme Court judge
Ketanji Brown Jackson (so cognitively challenged that she can't define
what a woman is, because, in her words, she's "not a biologist").*

Speaking of Ketanji Brown Jackson, rumor has it that they
asked her, "How many feet in a yard?" and she responded,
"How would I know, I'm not a podiatrist." [Laughter.]

Seriously, we could continue to discuss sociopolitical and sociocultural dialectics indefinitely. But since the focus of our
current series of discussions pertains to nonduality and Mind-
Only (and only to sociopolitics and socioculture in this context), we need to move on and leave further, more nuanced

BEYOND THE PHENOMENOLOGY OF SPIRIT, PART 4   153

consideration of my dialectical sociopolitical and sociocultural wheels to others with an abiding interest in the subject.

With this in mind, I'll conclude our discussion on the dialectical wheels with the following reminder: Duality and dialectical polarities are a reality in *Maya* (meaning our earthly plane of existence). And given that the World Spirit (through its mysterious workings in the current zeitgeist) has brought the dualistic dialectical polarities involving sociopolitics and socioculture to a seeming head, it must be realized, en masse, that no pseudo-spiritual, live-in-the-now mumbo-jumbo will provide the right synthesis to the thesis/antithesis of these polar oppositions (which are dividing us now as never before). Rather, it is only the national and global implementation of right-libertarian/ conservative principles that will do so.

CHAPTER FOURTEEN

Present-Day Nonduality and Mind-Only Teachings

Nonduality and Mind-Only Talking Heads

You're not the only person pontificating on nonduality and Mind-Only. What can you say about the prominent talking/writing heads who specialize in the subject?

Thanks to them, I was inspired to write my book on the subject.

So their words of wisdom led you to add yours to the subject.

No, it was their lack of wisdom, their inability to "crack the code" of the subject, that inspired me to "join the conversation," which necessarily entails critiquing their work. So, just presenting my own views without considering theirs doesn't do the subject justice.

So, just as you dissed all the other Kabbalah/Qabalah teachings, you're going to do the same to the current crop of prominent nonduality and Mind-Only philosophers.

That's right. In order, I'm going to briefly consider the words/works of Robert Wolfe, Rupert Spira, Bernardo Kastrup, Donald Hoffman, Jay Michaelson, and David Loy. Serious students and fans of nonduality and Mind-Only teachings will be familiar with most, if not all, of these fellows. My critiques and our discussion will necessarily be short, or else they could evolve into a book on their own. Let's get started.

Robert Wolfe has written a number of books pertaining to Advaita Vedanta teachings (which you can check out at Amazon). Several years ago, I read his text *Living Nonduality: Enlightenment Teachings of Self-realization* and wrote the following one-star Amazon review (which was eventually deleted by Amazon, along with my 300 + other book reviews).

My Review of *Living Nonduality* (Robert Wolfe)

Trailer-Trash Neo-Advaita Vedanta

[My 1-star review of *Living Nonduality: Enlightenment Teachings of Self-realization* by Robert Wolfe.]

I love reading and reviewing neo-Advaita Vedanta texts, because they are such a spiritual joke, they keep me in stitches. And this 480-page tome was good for at least a laugh a page.

At the beginning of the book, the author describes his "awakening." He had just separated from his wife and was living in a trailer, when he experienced a "sudden shift in perspective"—and presto! —he was enlightened. Was his sudden Self-realization attributable to years of intense *sadhana*? Heavens no, for as he avers, "I do not recommend meditation of any sort." In classic neo-Advaita speak, he simply informs us that "the spiritual quest came to an end."

In classic neo-Advaita Vedanta fashion, he doesn't detail his process of awakening, his awakening, or his awakened state. All he says is that his perspective shifted and he realized the "inseparability of all things." But, of course, that didn't pertain to his separation from his wife, though he asserts, "There cannot be any separation. Any!"

I repeatedly challenge these neo-Advaita Vedantans who preach absolute oneness and non-separation to practice what they preach by giving me unlimited access to their bank accounts and credit cards. So far, I've found no takers. And when I just tried to walk through the wall that separates me from my bedroom, I discovered a hard fact: the wall creates real separation, because unlike Superman, I couldn't penetrate it.

I could write my own tome deconstructing the neo-Advaita Vedanta nonsense permeating this text, but because this is just a review, I'll provide just a few samples, in quotes, from the text, followed by my comments.

"So what is your purpose in life? To do exactly what you're doing."

I'm sure that ISIS will be glad to learn that their purpose in life is to be doing what they're doing: murdering, raping, and torturing.

"Apart from false appearances, there is nothing."

In other words, this book is a false appearance, so how can it lead one to Truth?

"The core of the [Buddha's] entire teaching (his 45 years of it) is summarized in that one word: emptiness."

Emptiness is not the core of what the Buddha taught. It's the core of what the fogged-out father of Madhyamaka Buddhism, Nagarjuna, taught. Buddha himself made it clear that *Nirvana* is not emptiness, but the end of becoming, which is Being. The author further bastardizes the Buddha's teachings when he envisions him saying:

"Samsara and Nirvana are the same thing, in your mind: no experience by the individual, over a period of time. No individual, No experience, No time. No two things. No-thing."

Anyone familiar with the Buddha's teachings knows this is not what he taught. Moreover, in diametrical opposition to the author, who puts down meditation, the Buddha emphasized it as the core of his teachings. But, of course, the author doesn't mention this.

"We come from knowing nothing to knowing nothing."

In addition to this 480-page tome, the author has written several other books. One can only imagine how many books he would have written if he actually knew something.

I wish I could add "no stars" to the author's "No individual. No experience. No time. No two things. No-thing." But since I can't, I'll exercise the Great Compassion of a Buddha and generously give this book one star more than it deserves.

Wow! You pulled no punches in your review. But the 115 Amazon reviews of his book are mainly 5 stars.

The (clued-in) horns are few, and the (clueless) fur is many. Since Wolfe is the bottom of the nondual barrel and not worth further discussion, we'll move on to uber-popular Advaita Vedanta pundit Rupert Spira.

My Review of *The Transparency of Things* (Rupert Spira)

Rupert Spira was a student of Francis Lucille, even penning a book with him. Lucille, like me for a time, was a student of the late Advaita Vedanta guru Jean Klein. I discussed spirituality at length with him at a Jean Klein retreat 30 years ago, and our views differed significantly. I think the only thing we agreed upon was that Ramesh Balsekar (then a prominent Advaita Vedanta guru) was not "fully cooked."

I read Spira's book *The Transparency of Things* ten years ago and wrote the following (since deleted by Amazon) review of it:

Dumbed-down Daism Meets Dry, Lifeless Advaita Vedanta

[My 3-star review of *The Transparency of Things: The Nature of Experience* by Rupert Spira and Peter Russell.]

When I started reading this book, I was initially impressed with it—which is saying a lot, because after forty years of practicing, studying, and teaching esoteric spirituality, very little I read nowadays impresses me. But by the time I had finished it, my opinion of it had lessened considerably.

What impressed me initially was Spira's deep grasp of Advaita Vedanta and his seeming "upgrade" of its exclusive-reductive philosophy by integrating it with portions of Daism and Tibetan Dzogchen/Mahamudra. Although Spira doesn't mention Adi Da's Daism and Tibetan Dzogchen/Mahamudra by name, anyone who has studied these traditions will recognize his "expropriation" of them. Also, as an author myself, I was impressed with Spira's writing ability. The man writes clearly, concisely, and euphonically.

As I moved through the book, however, I began to see Spira's limitations as both a writer and a thinker. Although Spira, a wordsmith, writes seamlessly, his writings, over the course of the book, became a circumscribed drone. By the end of the book, I was tired of his repetitive philosophical considerations of consciousness, the 'I,' and epistemology. What started out as promising discourse never developed further or deeper. Instead, it was the same dry, pedantic arguments over and over in slightly varied contexts.

Prior to reading this book, I had "subjected" myself to Greg Goode's books *Direct Awareness* and *Standing as Awareness*, and I was glad to be done with Goode's obsession with Advaita epistemology (which I don't embrace); then I moved on to Spira's book, only to be subjected to more of the same (though not to the extent in Goode's books). When you read Ramana Maharshi or Nisargadatta Maharaj, the emphasis is on ontology, on waking up as Being, not on epistemology; but Advaita "head-trippers," such as Goode and Spira, seem to delight in considering the relation between cognition and conventional reality.

A major weakness of this book is its lack of "verticality." For instance, even though Spira periodically apes Adi Da's Dharma relative to Consciousness, he totally ignores it relative to Energy (*Shakti*, or Spirit). Spira is all *Siva*—but Truth is *Siva-Shakti*, not just static Awareness. Moreover, unlike Adi Da and Ramana Maharshi, he never ventures into esoteric anatomy, ignoring deep subjects such as the function of the Heart and the *Amrita Nadi* in the Self-realization process.

To illustrate the limitations of a *Siva*-only Dharma, consider Spira's statement, "What it is that brings about this Self-recognition [Self-realization] is a mystery." Unbeknownst to Spira, it's not a mystery: *Shakti*, Divine Power, the Higher *Kundalini*, severs one's Heart-knot, the final mortal coil, and unites with contracted *Siva* (the human soul) in the Heart-center (the *Hridayam*, not the *anahata* heart *chakra*), facilitating one's En-Light-enment, or Self-recognition. Few Advaitans understand that the relationship between *Siva* (Consciousness) and *Shakti* (Light-Energy) is dyadic, not dual. And until more of them understand this, Advaitans such as Spira will continue to produce dry, juiceless philosophy texts.

Bernardo Kastrup's Analytic Idealism

Rupert Spira and Bernardo Kastrup are buds, and both of them profess to hold almost identical views regarding Mind-Only and nonduality. If dry, juiceless, de-esotericized Mind-Only/nonduality philosophy in the language of Hindu Advaita Vedanta floats your boat, then you might vibe with Spira's writings and the numerous YouTube videos featuring him. And if a dry, academic Western presentation on the subject by a thinker with a PhD in both computer science and philosophy tickles your fancy, then by all means read Kastrup and watch his YouTube videos.

I've read Kastrup's book *The Idea of the World* and watched numerous YouTube videos wherein he repeats the core tenets of his Mind-Only philosophy, which he terms "analytic idealism." As you'll see, I not only have little regard for Kastrup's idealism, but little regard for him as a thinker in general.

Before I begin my critical dissection of Kastrup's idealism, I'll present two additional reasons (and there are others) why I hold him in low esteem as a thinker. First off, a la Sam Harris, he suffers from severe Trump Derangement Syndrome and has no appreciation of the MAGA movement. Here's what he's written about Trump:

> Donald Trump is a pathologically narcissistic, dangerously manipulative, clinically sociopathic and conspicuously unintelligent individual whose sole priority is himself, and who has no scruples about lying through his teeth so to deceive and use millions of people for the sole sake of his own personal agenda.

> I find it incomprehensible that Trump's supporters do not see that Trump is playing them, using them, exclusively for Trump's own pathological self-interest. It's all about Trump, not at all about his supporters, who are just manipulated means to an end. That's so plain it hurts.

Amazingly, when I Googled "Bernardo Kastrup on Joe Biden," I couldn't find a single word of criticism. Gee, I wonder why. Seriously, given how much Kastrup writes on sociopolitics, the implication (especially given his disdain for Trump) is that he has no major problem with the tyrannical, uber-corrupt Biden regime. Only a brainwashed Deep State-supporting leftoid who blogs on sociopolitics would not be blatantly critical of Biden's banana republic Marxist-Fascist reign.

Second, Kastrup buys into the non-existent climate-change crisis. He writes, "Human-induced climate change, together with nuclear war, are the two greatest threats to civilization today." Along with other percipient thinkers (including political whiz Vivek Ramaswamy) who have delved into the subject, I not only reject the idea of civilization-threatening manmade climate change, but also the idea of dire consequences resulting from non-human-induced global warming. In short, regarding sociopolitics (and sociopolitical philosophy), I consider Kastrup an ignoramus.

Now to my brief consideration of Kastrup's analytic idealism. Kastrup posits a universal mind, or unbound consciousness, as the substrate or primitive (his term) of existence. And matter or the physical universe to him is nothing more than an excitation (his term) or abstraction (his term) of mind. And in accordance with his interpretation of quantum theory, he contends that "all physical quantities are created by observation." In his words, "Observation is the physical world—not merely a representation of the world." Per Kastrup, "The physical properties of the world exist only insofar as they are perceptually experienced."

And how does Kastrup view humans and other living organisms in this "mental universe"? He writes:

We, as well as all other living organisms, are dissociated alters [parts or identities] of this unbound consciousness. The universe we see around us is the extrinsic appearance of phenomenality surrounding—but dissociated from—our alter. The living organisms we share the world with are the extrinsic appearances of other dissociated alters.

Kastrup also applies neo-Kantian creed in his idealist paradigm to explain how humans interface with phenomenal reality. He likens humans to airplane pilots using instruments to fly in bad weather. Like the pilots, we humans cannot see (perceive) the world outside us directly, as it is, but must navigate it through the medium of our limited sense "instruments," which enable us, like a blind man with a seeing-eye dog, to somehow function in the world.

What can you say about your idealist philosophy versus Kastrup's?

As made clear in all our previous discussions, I, like Kastrup, hold that a universal (or all-pervading) Mind, or Consciousness, is the all-subsuming Ground of the totality of manifest existents. Beyond this common agreement, my metaphysics, epistemology, and phenomenology are fundamentally antithetical to his. In other words, my views on how this universal Mind, or ultimate Reality, manifests and interfaces with conditional reality differ diametrically from his.

Because, up until this point, our ongoing series of Mind-Only/nonduality discussions has essentially been an elaboration of my idealist paradigm, it would be a gross detour from our current discussion (which focuses on others' paradigms) to restate my whole thesis here. Though I will be referring to aspects of it in the course of our current discussion, those not familiar with it should check it out in its entirety, so they can then intelligently compare it with other idealist paradigms that interest them.

Now, I'll begin my brief analysis of Kastrup's analytic idealism, which, for the most part, is built upon a spurious foundation of quantum theory that I reject. Hence, because I categorize this foundation and the conclusions that Kastrup derives from it as "quantum crapola," my analysis of his idealism, as you shall see, is less than favorable.

In his book *The Idea of the World*, wherein Kastrup expounds his idealist paradigm, the primary basis for his conclusions derives from his application of renowned physicist Carlo Rovelli's relational quantum mechanics (RQM) as support for his thesis. RQM (which is an interpretation of quantum mechanics) rejects the idea that reality depends upon the presence of a conscious observer. Its point is that reality is relational and that the state of a system can be described in relation to any physical object. Because RQM has nothing to do with consciousness or conscious observers, I reject Kastrup's application of it to support his thesis. I contacted Professor Rovelli by email, and herewith is our exchange, wherein he seconds my rejection:

> Greetings Dr. Rovelli,
>
> I just finished reading Professor Bernardo Kastrup's book *The Idea of the World: A Multi-Disciplinary Argument for the Mental Nature of Reality*, and I also watched the YouTube video "Quantum Physics and the End of Reality," which features you, Eric Weinstein, and Sabine Hossenfelder considering QM and reality. Please correct me if I'm wrong, but from the video, I gather that you believe in objective reality (that the moon is still there if no one observes/ perceives it), and that you state that your RQM interpretation of quantum mechanics has nothing to do with consciousness and conscious observers, just physical systems. Kastrup, on the other hand, applies RQM to support his metaphysical idealism argument that consciousness, or

mind, is the only reality, that "the physical properties of the world exist only insofar as they are perceptually perceived… Observation is the world - not merely a representation of the physical world… [QM] only predicts the unfolding of perception. In the absence of non-contextuality and realism, the 'physical world' of the relational interpretation is the contents of perception."

From my perspective, it seems that you don't agree with Kastrup's argument for the "mental nature of reality," nor with his application of RQM to support his thesis. Because I am now writing my own book on metaphysical idealism, which will include a consideration of Kastrup's argument (which I don't second), and cite you, I want to get clear on your view of his application of RQM to support his thesis.

I look forward to your reply.

Best Regards,

L. Ron Gardner

Here is Rovelli's reply:

Yes, you have it exactly right.

RQM, as I understand it, has nothing to do with conscious observers, and even less with a "mental nature of reality".

The physicists (like me) say that "velocity is relative," and use a language like "velocity is relative to an observer".

Then they say "the velocity of Jupiter relative to Saturn".

But it is a misunderstanding to deduce from this language that the physicists attribute consciousness or mental states to Saturn…

This is the mistake I detect in Kastrup's reading of RQM.

It remains true that RQM questions a naive materialism with an ontology of elements of matter bearing of properties.

Physics does so. In RQM, properties are relational. But from that to a strong argument for idealism the jump seems too large to me.

carlo

Wow! That blows a HUGE hole in Kastrup's work, because he's big on applying Rovelli's RQM to support his analytic idealism. How about Kastrup's other applications of QM to his work?

All BS. There is zero proof that any of Kastrup's QM-based assertions he applies to support his analytic idealism have any validity. But because pinhead academics, such as Kastrup and his bud Donald Hoffman (next on our agenda to consider), lack the gnosis and philosophical chops to apply esoteric spirituality to their theses, they resort to the "low-hanging fruit"—quantum crapola—in their attempts to legitimize their pseudo-scientific, philosophically flawed work.

Kastrup, laughably, says that the world's "measurable physical proper-ties do not exist before being observed" and that "observation boils down to perceived experience."

Yep, a total joke. If the tree falls in the forest and no one is there to hear it fall, it still makes a sound. If you wake up in the middle of the night and, still half-asleep, unconsciously stumble into the wall (which you neither observed nor per-ceived) and crack your head open, that is proof the wall exists exclusive of your consciousness.

Where does Kastrup go wrong?

In numerous places—too many for us to consider them all in our brief analysis of his work—but in this case, where he errs is by not comprehending that existence (physical reality) has primacy over consciousness in *Maya* (measured-out phenomenal reality). Hence, manifest existence exists prior to, and independent of, observers. When someone can go to Vegas and, through their mind-power, control the roll of the dice, I'll reconsider my POV.

I'm neither a physicist (I had a year of physics in college 50 + years ago, prior to the Standard Model, and I've forgotten 50 +% of what I learned) nor a philosopher of science (like the popular Tim Maudlin); but I'm no dummy, and after having watched numerous educational physics videos at YouTube, I now recognize quantum crapola when I see it.

And speaking of quantum crapola and Maudlin, watch the short YouTube video "Bernardo Kastrup/Tim Maudlin: Non-Locality, Bell's Theorem" at the YouTube channel Curt Jaimungal. In this video, Maudlin, a professor who specializes in the philosophy of science, quickly and cuttingly dismisses Kastrup's idealism because it denies physical reality, yet depends on physical experiments as its basis for validation. The video is short, because after Maudlin confronts him with this contradiction, Kastrup, in a huff, exits the debate.

In the video, Kastrup contends that the 2022 Nobel Prize disproves local reality and physical realism, whereas Maudlin holds that it refutes local realism but not physical realism.

Actually, the 2022 Nobel Prize only refutes local realism if the wave function is real and not just a mathematical abstraction. Erwin Schrodinger himself, the Nobel Prize winning physicist (1933) renowned for originating the Schrodinger equation, which gives the evolution of a wave function over time, mocked the idea that quantum theory, which is based on probabilistic superposition (meaning that subatomic particles, prior to measurement and the supposed wave-function collapse, exist in indeterminate states that are "neither here nor there or both here and there") applies to the real world. To express his disdain for what he considered a gross misunderstanding and misapplication of quantum mechanics, he posited his famous Schrodinger's Cat thought experiment [Google it for a full description], which makes a mockery of the idea of superposition on a macro scale, because it, most absurdly, means that the cat in the box must be simultaneously dead and alive until its real state is revealed upon "measurement" (when the box is opened).

Maudlin himself fails to understand that the line separating locality and non-locality is blurred because there is no real entanglement (or causal, or "spooky," action) between particles separated at a distance; there is only correlative information (such as knowing the spin direction of one particle of a pair based on that of the other). Hence, the distinction between local and non-local realism is a tenuous one.

Maudlin rightly contradicts Kastrup by making it clear that the 2022 Nobel Prize does not rule out superdeterminism (meaning hidden-variables theories that replace probabilistic quantum mechanics with versions of deterministic mechanics that yield the same measurement results). An example of such a deterministic theory is the pilot-light theory, also known as Bohmian mechanics. A more recent example is Harvard professor Jacob Barandes's Stochastic-Quantum Correspondence, which rejects the wave function.

For links to more hidden-variables theories that yield the same predictions as QM, check out esteemed physicist Sabine Hossenfelder's excellent YouTube video "Why Is Quantum Mechanics Non-Local?" Hossenfelder, like Rovelli and Maudlin, has little regard for Kastrup's QM-based idealism.

The bottom line regarding quantum theory is that, although it remains canon because it efficiently yields very accurate predictions and measurements, it is (as iconic physicist Roger Penrose makes clear) internally inconsistent; thus it is destined to be superseded by a theory that not only yields just as accurate results, but which is not an affront to the principle of causal determinism, which is germane to every other canonical theory in science.

But until quantum theory is supplanted as canon, opportunistic philosophers, such as Kastrup and his bud Donald Hoffman, will continue to exploit its anti-realist weirdness to promote their own anti-realist theories.

Kastrup says that "matter outside mind is not an empirical fact."

Kastrup's unclear writing creates confusion. In his book, he fails to capitalize "mind," which, in some places, blurs the distinction between impersonal, universal Mind (or Consciousness) and personal, individual mind (or consciousness). In the excerpt you quoted, he means universal Mind. Given that Mind is the illimitable, spaceless Substrate wherein all phenomena, including matter, arise, he is correct.

Kastrup contends that "The notion of dichotomy between mind and matter arises from language."

Whether Kastrup is referring to universal Mind or to individual mind, the distinction between either of them and matter has nothing to do with language and everything to do with real ontological differences. Only a philosopher as delusional as Kastrup could imagine that the difference between mind and matter is merely linguistic.

It seems that the area where your idealism most significantly differs from Kastrup's is that you accept, rather than deny, physical reality.

Yes. In accordance with Kashmir Shaivism, I view physical reality as real rather than an illusion. Moreover, unlike Kastrup's flat idealism, which is bereft of a dynamic dimension, I explain the continuum from Mind (or Consciousness) to physical reality via Clear-Light Energy (Mind's dynamic *Shakti*), which morphs into the full spectrum of stepped-down energies, some of which "crystallize" into matter.

Kastrup contends that "realism—the notion that there is an objective world—is meaningless." He asserts that "physical objective matter is not an observable fact."

There is no end Kastrup's disconnect from reality. My advice to him is this: Get your quantum-crapola ass on a scale, and the reading—shocking as it may be—will convince you that the physical matter you animate is an observable, measurable fact.

Kastrup claims that "The physical world we perceive isn't merely discovered by observation, but created by it."

I've got news for Kastrup: his, or anybody else's, observations can't create jack shit. Whatever world Kastrup lives in, it has little do with the real world.

To sum, Kastrup's stilted highbrow academese and quantum-crapola analytic idealism will bedazzle the philosophic ignoranti, but the gnostic cognoscenti will patently reject it.

The Case Against Donald Hoffman

As delusional as Bernardo Kastrup is with regard to reality, Donald Hoffman, UC Irvine professor of cognitive psychology, is perhaps even more so. Together, these two leading academic "lights" on quantum-crapola idealism have become uber-popular icons for those who worship at the altar of anti-reality.

To those in the know, the first evidence that Hoffman is philosophically challenged is his adoration of fogged-out pop guru Eckhart Tolle, his primary spiritual influence. If Hoffman didn't live in a spiritual-intellectual bubble, he'd know about and have read my book *Beyond the Power of Now: A Guide to, and Beyond, Eckhart Tolle's Teachings,* which not only deconstructs the rampant poppycock permeating Tolle's magnum opus *The Power of Now*, but presents spiritual Dharma on a level a quantum leap beyond Tolle's text.

In addition to his infatuation with Tolle, Hoffman also vibes with *A Course in Miracles*, a second-rate quasi-Christian mysticism course that should be titled "A Course in Spiritual Trash," which anybody steeped in real Christian mysticism would toss into a garbage bin or donate to a local Goodwill store. If Hoffman were a deep, serious spiritual seeker interested in true, esoteric Christian mysticism, he would have come across my seminal text *Electrical Christianity: A Revolutionary Guide to Jesus' Teachings and Spiritual Enlightenment* and found it immensely more enlightening than *A Course in Miracles*.

What can you say about Hoffman's book The Case Against Reality?

After watching numerous YouTube interviews with Hoffman and hearing his same full-of-bull anti-reality shtick over and over, I had zero interest in reading his book; so I didn't.

The truth is, Hoffman had no business writing a book titled *The Case Against Reality* because he doesn't even know what reality is. Unbeknownst to him, reality is simply that which exists. Regardless of the ontological status of an existent, simply by virtue of existing, it is real. In other words, there is no case against reality; there is only the question of the ontological status of the various existents that constitute it.

Hoffman holds that consciousness is foundational and can't be booted up from space-time and matter. While I concur with that idealist assessment, I disagree with virtually every postulation he makes based on it. First and foremost, the fact that consciousness (or Consciousness) is Ultimate Reality does not render phenomenal reality (space-time and objects in it) unreal or an illusion, as Hoffman contends. Nothing unreal can come from the Real, so the fact that phenomenal reality (space-time existence) derives from Ultimate Reality (the spaceless, timeless Existent, or Consciousness) does not negate its reality.

Hoffman not only negates the reality of reality, but the ability of humans to perceive veridical reality. He employs three principal arguments in his attempt to undermine the efficacy of man's perceptual faculty.

The first (through the work of his mathematician-partner) is his implementation of evolutionary game theory, which, he claims, proves that evolution hid the truth from mankind, that there is zero percent chance humans evolved to perceive reality, and 100 percent chance they evolved for fitness concerns, merely to maximize perpetuation of their genes. To this, I say evolutionary game theory is hardly infallible or necessarily robust. Without resorting to "lost-in-math" game-theory analysis (which also serves to perpetuate climate-change myths), no clear-thinking individual would buy the idea that Darwinian evolution has in no way fostered man's desire and ability to perceive reality; rather, such an individual would conclude that man's ability to perceive reality is inextricably linked to his reproductive fitness.

Hoffman's second principal argument attempts to prove that human sense-perception is defective, but what it proves instead is that Hoffman, despite his PhD in cognitive psychology, is an epistemological ignoramus. In some of his YouTube videos, he provides examples of optical illusions that putatively discredit the validity of our senses. This is specious for the following reasons: First, although our five senses are limited in scope and precision, they (along with sensory extensions, such as microscopes and telescopes) do what they are intended to do: inform us that something exists. It is then up to the "sixth sense," the mind, to properly identify the contents of our either direct or instrument-enhanced sense-perceptions. For example, we might initially see a piece of rope and mistake it for a snake; but upon further analysis, we properly identify it as a piece of rope. Second, if our senses are invalid, producers of only illusion, then our minds, which are built upon our sense-perceptions, are also invalid, thereby rendering any ideas anyone has of a sensible world as folly.

Hoffman's third principal argument that putatively impugns man's ability to perceive veridical reality centers on space-time as a deluding universal interface. Space-time, according to Hoffman, can be likened to a video game wherein one's attention is completely captured by the sights and sounds of the game, while being oblivious to the underlying hardware, software, and electronics that comprise its more fundamental reality. For example, per Hoffman, when you're playing Grand Theft Auto, you think that you're actually turning the steering wheel with your joy stick, but in reality, it's the game's (hidden from you) "guts" responsible for the ostensible redirection of the apparent car. But this argument/analogy doesn't impugn man's ability to perceive reality; it simply identifies his attention as selective. If a player needed to get into the underlying guts of the game to play it, he would; but when he plays this game, or the "game of life," and doesn't need to look below the surface, why should he devote the extra time and energy to do so?

It seems like Hoffman equates space-time with Maya.

Yep, and so do I. But he errs in his understanding of *Maya*, which literally means that which has been "measured out" from the Immeasurable (meaning Mind, or Consciousness). What is measured out from Mind is physically, phenomenally real, and not an illusion, as Hoffman erroneously contends. And once the universe of space-time existents has been measured out from Mind, regardless of what new shapes or forms the raw, emanated existents might take, they do not need to be measured or perceived or observed to manifest objective physical qualities. And unbeknownst to Hoffman, man's cognitive faculties, which he disses, are valid instruments for directly perceiving and recognizing this reality.

Hoffman not only denigrates space-time, reducing it to an illusory interface, but he goes even further, insisting that "space-time is doomed."

Yes, he seconds physicist Nima Arkani-Hamed's statement that "space-time is doomed." Beyond heat-death through entropy, Arkani-Hamed speculates that space-time may be doomed from giant particle colliders (such as the Large Hadron Collider) that produce ever-higher energy collisions of protons which could imperil the universe as we know it by creating black holes whose gravity is so strong they can suck in planets and even stars. Most physicists, however, scoff at this notion.

But beyond his secondary "doom-through-black-holes" hypothesis, the primary reason Arkani-Hamed believes space-time is doomed pertains to its non-fundamentality. He contends that he has identified static geometric structures, called "decorated permutations," which exist outside (and beyond) space-time, and thus are more fundamental than it is. Hence, metaphorically speaking, four-dimensional space-time (as the foundation of reality) is doomed.

Donald Hoffman not only buys into Arkani-Hamed's decorated-permutations paradigm, he also claims that he's working on a dynamical aspect to them.

Do you buy into Arkani-Hamed's paradigm?

No, I say that Donald Hoffman and Nima Arkani-Hamed are full of hooey, and I challenge anyone to argue otherwise. The fact that Hoffman claims to be working on a dynamical aspect to the putatively static Amplituhedron (the most prominent decorated permutation) and other supposed geometrical structures outside space-time is laughable, because no such structures exist. They are, in fact, mere conceptual models used to simplify quantum computations.

Arkani-Hamed's Amplituhedron encodes amplitudes (building blocks of probabilities in particle physics) in the "area" of a multi-dimensional analog of a polyhedron (hence, Amplituhedron). But there is no such thing as "the Amplituhedron," meaning a monolithic geometric structure outside space-time that is more fundamental than space-time. Therefore, "the Amplituhedron" is just a concept, which manifests in various amplituhedra, each corresponding to a calculation one might make. The Amplituhedron's advantage is that it makes these calculations much simpler. But this hardly makes the Amplituhedron more fundamental or foundational than quantum mechanics or space-time. Imagine using an abacus as a computational tool and then discovering an electronic calculator that is many times faster. Well, that is an analogy for what Arkani-Hamed has done. And while it's commendable, it hardly revolutionizes physics, as he and others contend, but merely simplifies quantum computations.

Even though Hoffman believes that decorated permutations are more fundamental than space-time, he still considers consciousness as most fundamental.

He's wrong about decorated permutations, which are just mental abstractions, but right about the fundamentality of consciousness. Unfortunately, along with his failure to grok space-time, he also lacks a deep understanding of universal consciousness, which, unbeknownst to him, is Di-"vine" in nature, consisting not only of the "vine" of Mind, but also the "vine" of Spirit, or Clear-Light-Energy, which "crystallizes" into stepped-down, manifest forms of energy and matter. Hence, in addition to being an epistemological ignoramus, he is also a spiritual one.

Anything more you want to add to your "case against Donald Hoffman"?

In addition to being an epistemological and spiritual ignoramus, Hoffman is also an ontological one, possessing scant understanding of levels and states of consciousness and reality. On top of the Arkani-Hamed quantum crapola he peddles through the medium of decorated permutations, Hoffman also promotes the same anti-realist quantum crapola as Bernardo Kastrup, meaning he doesn't believe that space-time objects exist when they're not perceived. According to him, there is no moon in the sky without someone to see it; according to me, that makes him—pardon the term—a lunatic.

Everything Is God (Jay Michaelson)

Given that Jay Michaelson's book—*Everything Is God: The Radical Path of Nondual Judaism*—pertains to both nonduality and Judaism, it was a must-read for me. I'll be following up my *Nonduality and Mind-Only* book with one on Kabbalah, and I was eager to see how Michaelson elaborates nondual Judaism.

Before diving into Michaelson's book, I Googled him and learned that he is very learned (JD from Yale and a PhD in Jewish Thought from the Hebrew University of Jerusalem)—and very brainwashed (and brainless) sociopolitically. He's written for leftist rags (including *Rolling Stone*, *The Daily Beast*, and *The Washington Post*) and been featured on leftist "fake news" channels (CNN, MSNBC). He suffers from severe Trump Derangement Syndrome; and from the online articles of his that I read, I learned how politically clueless and deluded he is. Upon realizing that Michaelson was a cognitively challenged libtard, I didn't expect to find much, if any, unique and profound wisdom in his book—and upon reading it, I didn't. What I found was the same exoteric nondual teachings (and nonsense) that permeate all the other contemporary works I've encountered on the subject.

When you told me you were going to discuss it, I got a copy, and unsurprisingly, I second your assessment of it.

That's good. Now, before I get into the nondual teachings, I want to touch upon the Marxist ideology that colors Michaelson's writing. Here's a quote from his book:

> We are used to boundaries, and as Ken Wilber has said, every boundary is a battle line—the most intuitive is the most destructive. The moment you establish a boundary between what is mine and what is yours, we at once fly in the face of ecological interdependence and perpetuate the objectification and exploitation that our hyperdualistic culture has brought about… Our human tendency to dualize, hierarchize, reduce, and despoil is where our delusion begins and ends…

> My supposed need for security, home, hearth, is a late capitalist, bourgeois affection conditioned by nineteenth-and twentieth-century advertising and cultural production.

What Michaelson fails to understand is that without individual property rights, man becomes a slave to the State. Ayn Rand explains:

The right to life is the source of all rights—and the right to property is their only implementation. Without property rights, no other rights are possible. Since man has to sustain his life by his own effort, the man who has no right to the product of his effort has no means to sustain his life. The man who produces while others dispose of his product is a slave.

In addition to Marxism, postmodern drivel also pollutes his writing.

Very true. In addition to his attack on man's rights and sovereignty, Michaelson also demeans man's consciousness, reducing it to what he terms a "meme complex." He writes:

Consciousness is really made up of memes, units of information that replicate themselves, a bit like genetic information does… [Regarding consciousness], a postmodernist would reply: yes, the thought arose—but that doesn't mean there was a "you" thinking it. There was just a set of memes thinking the thought, interpreting it, and constructing a self on the basis of it.

It's hard to believe that anyone could be so clueless as to think that memes can think, interpret thoughts, and construct a self.

Not when you realize the progressive brain rot caused by "progressive" Marxist and postmodern ideology, which have taken over Michaelson's brain—like a meme. [Laughter.]

Michaelson writes: "As Ken Wilber has written, we can now for the first time in history, 'put it all on the table'—the 'sum total of human knowledge … the knowledge, experience, wisdom, and reflections of all major human civilizations.'"

Yep, and like Wilber, whom he vibes with, Michaelson is incapable of sifting through the "sum total of human knowledge" and identifying the foremost spiritual and sociopolitical teachings. And like Wilber, Michaelson is bereft of an esoteric dimension, never moving beyond a superficial, topical consideration of what is now "on the table" for philosophers and exegetes to consider in these fields.

For example, the subtitle of Michaelson's book is "The Radical Path of Nondual Judaism," yet the book is devoid of an explication of not only the Kabbalistic Tree of Life and the Sefirot (meaning the theosophical Kabbalah), but also the practice of connecting to and receiving the Supernal Influx (meaning the mystical Kabbalah). In other words, the subtitle is a joke, because the book isn't a "radical" (or gone-to-the-root) text on nondual Jewish mysticism, but just another superficial perennial philosophy text that identifies the common theme of nondualism in multiple spiritual traditions.

Because I don't want to spend undue time deconstructing the whole of Michaelson's book, I'm simply going to critique select statements from it that are contrary to my own nondual spiritual philosophy.

On the page prior to the Contents page, Michaelson provides two epigraphs that exemplify his nondual philosophy. The first, by R. Yitzhak Isaac of Homel, is: "There is nothing but God alone, and, once again, all is God."

This statement mirrors the title of Michaelson's book, *Everything Is God*. As I've repeatedly made clear in our discussions, everything is NOT God. If your BM is God, why flush it down the toilet? And if it's God, it should be able to create a universe. But sadly, turds can't create even a single cockroach. And more sadly, libturds, such as Michaelson, can't create even a single impressive work of philosophy.

The second epigraph, by Allen Ginsberg, reads: "The World is holy! The skin is holy! The nose is holy!… Everything is holy! Everybody's holy! Everywhere holy!"

Unbeknownst to Michaelson and the late, famous Beat poet Ginsberg, nothing created is holy (or sacred), because everything created is a temporary space-time appearance destined to disappear. Only the uncreated, timeless Holy One (including His Holy Spirit and Holy Christ/Son/Self/Buddha) is truly Holy.

Didn't Ginsberg say something to the effect, "I saw the best minds of my generation rot"?

Yep, and it's the same thing I've seen happen to the best minds of my generation afflicted with the libtard virus. Michaelson, however, isn't stricken with just the libtard virus, but also the "Madhyamaka virus" (a term I've coined for the cognitive disease that afflicts those who abandon Aristotelian logic for Nagarjunian illogic).

Michaelson writes, "In nondual consciousness, the mountains are both: both everything and nothing, both existent and nonexistent." Actually, the mountains are neither everything and nothing, nor existent and nonexistent. They are simply existent as mountains. But for Michaelson, a sophist who mindlessly parrots Nagarjuna's nonsensical Madhyamaka philosophy, real ontological distinctions vanish in the nondual fog that envelops his brain.

Speaking of distinctions (or the lack thereof), Michaelson doesn't grasp the fundamental differences that exist between Hindu Yoga (including Vedanta) and Madhyamaka Buddhism (which, along with Marxism and postmodernism, warps his brain). He writes, "What the Vedantists call the Self (Atman), the Buddhists call non-self, and the Hasidim call the *ayin* are three perspectives of the same phenomenon: the egoless, timeless emptiness, the nothingness one finds when one looks for oneself." Unbeknownst to Michaelson, the Self (Atman) is not a phenomenon (a created existent or event), nor is it emptiness or nothingness (which are non-existents with no ontological status). The Self (Atman) is uncreated Consciousness itself, the Seer, which sees both forms/thing-ness and emptiness/nothingness (the absence of perceivable things). Emptiness can only be an object to the Subject, the Self, which is Sat-Cit-Ananda (Being-Consciousness-Bliss), not a non-existent nothingness.

Michaelson contends that God is both Being and Nothingness.

That's a blatant contradiction, because Being implies existence as some "Thing." And as Kashmir Shaivism makes clear, the "Thing" that Being (really the Supreme, or Di-"vine," Being) exists as is Consciousness-Spirit (*Siva-Shakti*).

Where Michaelson goes wrong (in addition to his many other errors) is by confusing Nothingness and No-thingness. Unbeknownst to him, *Ayin* does not mean Nothing; it means No-thing, meaning that God is not a created, phenomenal thing, but the uncreated, transcendental "Thing (or Being)-in-Itself." Something cannot come from nothing, but something, meaning the universe of existents, can, and does, come from Being, the "Thing" (or Consciousness-Spirit)-in-Itself.

Nothing Michaelson says makes sense. He talks about unitive and nondual consciousness, yet says, "Consciousness is a trick played by a well-functioning brain, the result of decades of data and millennia of genetic evolution." You can't have it both ways.

Michaelson is a contradiction-riddled clown. Unbeknownst to him, consciousness is neither a trick nor a set of memes. Rather, it is the changeless "Mental Substance," or Mind, un-derlying all phenomena. Michaelson is so clueless that he can't differentiate the mutable *content* of consciousness (memes, thoughts, emotions, etc.) from the immutable *context* that is consciousness. Here's an excerpt from his book that encapsulates his idiocy:

> But then, take science seriously, and remember that there is no self either: consciousness is an illusion of the brain, after all. Believe the postmodernists, the Buddhists, the Darwinists, the cognitive materialists, and the Hasidim when they say that this sense of ego, while essential for survival, causes us to mistake a pattern of phenomena for something that's actually there. Really, there is no soul, just a buzz of neurons. So no God, no self. And then … what?
>
> What's left, after the self is subtracted, is what nondualists mean by "God."

So, according to Michaelson, a human—a pseudo-self with a consciousness that is an illusion (just a product of memes) with no soul (just a buzz of neurons pretending to be one)—can, through self-subtraction, realize God, which is Nothing. But because, per Michaelson, a human, or pseudo-self, has no free will (as he claims elsewhere in his book), it has no way to consciously subtract itself.

There's seemingly no end to Michaelson's bad takes on spirituality and nonduality.

But there is an end to our critique of them. We've only scratched the surface of his bad spiritual/philosophical takes—and we could continue to expose and mock them ad nauseam. But why bother when it should already be clear that he's a clueless clown in a nondual circus of his own making. With this in mind, we'll now move on to our consideration of David R. Loy's book *Nonduality in Buddhism and Beyond*.

Nonduality in Buddhism and Beyond
(David R. Loy)

What can you say about Loy's book?

It's an interesting, though limited and flawed, consideration of nonduality. It's limited because, like Kastrup, Hoffman, and Michaelson, Loy doesn't consider the tantric traditions and the role of *Shakti*, or Light-Energy, in nonduality. He focuses mainly on Mahayana Buddhism (Madhyamaka, Yogacara, Zen), Vedantic Hinduism, and Taoism, and provides different, though related, ways to understand what nonduality means. His thesis is also flawed because, like Kastrup, Hoffman, and Michaelson, he is epistemically challenged, beset by arguments that don't accord with reality.

According to Loy, nonduality can be viewed in three principal ways: as 1) the negation of dualistic thinking, 2) the non-plurality of the world, and 3) the nondifference of subject and object. We'll consider each of these in order.

Negation of dualistic thinking is prevalent in Mahayana Buddhism. For example, in Madhyamaka (and some schools of Zen), one commonly (provisionally) attempts to negate dualistic distinctions by imagining all perceived things as empty. And in Yogacara (and some schools of Zen), one commonly attempts to negate distinctions by imagining separate objects as nothing but Mind. From this point of view, it is dualistic thinking that falsely differentiates things; and by undermining such thinking (by mentally resolving all distinctions into a single Whole of emptiness or Mind), one can free oneself from the bondage of duality. But the problem one runs into when negating dualistic thinking can be summarized in a single word—reality. No matter how hard one attempts to perceive everything as emptiness or Mind, real-world experience tells us otherwise. It informs us, often painfully, that separate space-time existents are a persistent, intractable reality. The unavoidable conclusion for the truth-seeker is that the negation of dualistic thinking cannot negate the dualistic reality of worldly existence.

How about nondual thinking that voids distinctions between opposites, such as good and evil or black and white?

Like all nondual thinking, it flies in the face of reality. Only someone utterly delusional or suffering from severe cognitive dissonance can't recognize clear-cut distinctions between good and evil and black and white. Nondual thinking is an affront to rational thinking, which is based on valid sense perception and logic, the non-contradictory identification of the facts of reality (including distinct, separate existents).

Loy's second principle sense, or category, of nonduality—the non-plurality of the world—is the one I resonate with. He describes it as each thing being "a manifestation of some indefinable substance," meaning an "underlying Monistic Ground," or "One Mind."

But Loy perceives this principle, as well as the first one, as incomplete. He writes:

> We have seen the connection between the first two dualities: it is because of our dualistic ways of thinking that we perceive the world pluralistically. The relationship between the corresponding nondualities is parallel: the world as a collection of discrete things (including me) in space and time is not something objectively given, which we merely observe passively; if our ways of thinking change, that world changes also for us. But there is still something lacking in this formulation. By itself it is incomplete, for it

leaves unclarified the relation between the subject and the nondual world that the subject experiences. It was stated earlier that the nondual whole is "spiritual" because the One Mind includes my mind, but how consciousness could be incorporated has not been explained. The world is not really experienced as a whole if the subject that perceives it is still separate from it in its observation of it. In this way the second sense of nonduality, conceived objectively, is unstable and naturally tends to evolve into a third sense. This third sense, like the other two, must be understood as a negation. The dualism denied is our usual distinction between subject and object, an experiencing self that is distinct from what is experienced, be it sense-object, physical action, or mental event. The corresponding nonduality is experience in which there is no such distinction between subject and object. However extraordinary and counterintuitive such nonduality may be, it is an essential element of many Asian systems (and some Western ones, of course). Since the primary purpose of this work is to analyze this third sense of nonduality, it is necessary to establish in detail the prevalence and significance of this concept.

So Loy, in essence, claims that the third sense of nonduality subsumes the other two, and thus is the only true or integral sense of nonduality.

Correct. He writes:

> What is most significant for us is that the third sense of nonduality, the nondifference between subject and object, was essential to all of them. (Hereafter, unless otherwise noted, the term nonduality will always refer to this third sense.)

He cites examples from Vedanta to support his claim, but makes it clear that other Asian philosophies also support his thesis:

This claim is by no means unique to Vedanta; it is found in virtually all the Asian philosophies that assert this third sense of nonduality: our experience not only can be but already is and always was nondual; any sense of a subject apart from that which is experienced is an illusion.

But you reject the Vedanta point of view.

Correct. Unlike Loy, I do not define *Maya* as illusion, but as phenomenal reality—and in phenomenal reality, subject-object duality is an incontrovertible fact. Moreover, none of Loy's citations regarding other Asian philosophies convincingly supports his claim for the nondifference between subject and object as the core tenet of nonduality. Let's consider a few of his citations, with the first being from Vasubandhu, one of the founders of Yogacara Buddhism:

> Through the attainment of the state of Pure Consciousness, there is the non-perception of the perceivable; and through the non-perception of the perceivable (i.e., the object) there is the non-acquisition of the mind (i.e., the subject). Through the non-perception of these two, there arises the realization of the Essence of Reality. Where there is an object there is a subject, but not where there is no object. The absence of an object results in the absence also of a subject, and not merely in that of grasping. It is thus that there arises the cognition which is homogeneous, without object, indiscriminate and supermundane. The tendencies to treat object and subject as distinct and real entities are forsaken, and thought is established in just the true nature of one's thought.

Although Vasubandhu, in order to realize the state of Pure Consciousness, treats object and subject as non-distinct, this does not negate their fundamental distinctness. His negation of their distinctness is merely provisional; for once you begin to interact with the phenomenal world, the reality of subject-object separation will confront you. For example, if you walk into a wall and break your nose, the wall as a separate and distinct object apart from your bodymind (the subject) will literally "hit you in the face."

Loy writes:

> More recently, the Italian scholar Giuseppe Tucci has summarized the final objective of Tibetan Buddhist soteriology as follows: "Higher cognition is the penetrating to, and cognizing of, the true nature of these appearances, of these forms created by our discursive knowledge, these products of a false dichotomy between subject and object. . . The final objective remains the awakening of that higher cognition, that shes rab, Sanskrit prajna, in the adept's consciousness, which enables him to survey the ultimate nature of all things with the clarity of direct insight; in other words, the transcending of the subject-object dichotomy."

Contrary to Loy and Tucci, these "forms created by our discursive knowledge" are not created by our discursive knowledge, but are properly identified by it. They aren't products of a "false dichotomy between subject and object," but rather the recognition of the reality of this dichotomy. Unbeknownst to Loy and Tucci, identification of the ultimate nature of all things does not negate subject-object duality, but transcends it.

Loy cites renowned Zen scholar D. T. Suzuki for support of his non-difference-of-subject-and-object thesis:

> In his voluminous writings on Zen, D. T. Suzuki repeatedly emphasized that the satori experience is the realization of nonduality. For example, in the first series of his Essays on Zen Buddhism, during a discussion of "original Mind," he states that "there is no separation between knower and

known." Zen is "the unfolding of a new world hitherto un-perceived in the confusion of the dualistically-trained mind."

To anyone with even a jot of epistemological sophistication, it couldn't be clearer that there is separation between knower (subject) and known (object). The individual knower and the known object exist independently of each other. If one is re-moved, the other still exists. Moreover, there is also separation between an individual knower and his knowledge, because others can possess the same knowledge, exclusive of the indi-vidual knower.

I could continue to deconstruct other citations by Loy in support of his third sense of nonduality, but that would be pointless, because they are just more of the same as the ones I've critiqued. Instead, I want to briefly consider two other nondualities which Loy claims are closely related.

So, although Loy identifies three senses or principles of nonduality, he adds yet another two to his consideration.

That's right. Regarding these two nondualities, he writes:

> [In my book] there will be occasion to consider two other non-dualities which are closely related: first, what has been called the identity of phenomena and Absolute, or the Mahayana equation of samsara and nirvana, which can also be expressed as "the nonduality of duality and nonduality"; second, the pos-sibility of a mystical unity between God and man.

Regarding the first of these two nondualities, Loy writes:

> My approach supports the Mahayana claim that samsara is nirvana. There is only one reality—this world, right here and now—but this world may be experienced in two dif-ferent ways. Samsara is the relative, phenomenal world as usually experienced, which is delusively understood to

consist of a collection of discrete objects (including "me") that interact causally in space and time. Nirvana is that same world but as it is in itself, nondually incorporating both subject and object into a whole.

Unfortunately, Loy doesn't understand *samsara* and *Nirvana*. *Samsara* is the time-bound cycle of *becoming*, of successive changes of state, including that of birth and death. *Nirvana*, timeless *Being*, is the end of *samsara*. Gautama Buddha did NOT teach that *samsara* is *Nirvana*. He, rightly, taught that *samsara* is suffering, and that *Nirvana* is escape from *samsaric* suffering. What is born and changes—appearing and disappearing—is not the same as That which is unborn and changeless—the Realm of *Nirvana*.

Even if one equates the Realm of *Nirvana* with God (or Mind), God's (or Mind's) *samsaric* creation (a.k.a. *Maya*) is not eternal, immutable God or Mind, but ephemeral, mutable phenomena destined to cycle from dust to dust.

The second of Loy's two add-on senses of nonduality pertains to, in his words, "mystical unity between God and man." He considers this subject in the context of the Bhagavad Gita and asks the following question: Is a nondual relationship between God and man possible? And he answers that it is, that the dualism in theism can transform from a dualistic to a nondualistic mode when the mystic's consciousness merges with universal Consciousness, the Absolute.

Do you concur with Loy's answer?

Many mystics, particularly those in the Hindu tradition, who attain God-union claim to be God. Their common refrain is "I Am That." But mystics in other traditions who attain God-union usually maintain the dualistic (and thus ontological) distinction between themselves and the Deity. I side with the latter. When I see mystics equating their ontological status with God's, I roll my eyes, because I don't buy it.

Can you contrast your nonduality philosophy with Loy's?

The essence of Loy's nonduality philosophy is, in his words, "nondifference between subject and object." As made clear in our discussion, I do not subscribe to Loy's nonduality philosophy; I subscribe to Kashmir Shaivism's, which Loy, sadly, doesn't even consider.

Per Kashmir Shaivism, all things are a manifestation of *Siva*, Consciousness (or Mind) itself, and the phenomenal world (including subject-object duality) is real, existing and having its being in Consciousness. *Siva*, the One Mind, has become everything; hence there is "top-down" nonduality, with Consciousness subsuming all existents. However, although *Siva* has manifested as all existents, all existents are not timeless, immutable *Siva*, but time-bound, mutable derivatives stemming from Him, who is never implicated in His "cosmic dance" of creation. So, from the "bottom-up" perspective of phenomenal reality, which includes separate conscious agents in space and time, subject-object duality is reality.

Once *Maya* (phenomenal reality) is "measured out" from Immeasurable *Siva*, duality pervades the cosmos. In other words, although *Siva* has become all things, all things are not *Siva*. All things are in, and of, *Siva*, the "Mental Ground and Substance" of the universe; but, again, that does not make them *Siva*.

Unlike you, Loy doesn't account for Shakti *as the dynamic aspect of* Siva, *the One Mind (or Consciousness).*

Where Loy, as well Kastrup, Hoffman, and Michaelson, grossly miss the boat in their respective paradigms is illustrated by the following meme I saw posted at Facebook: "Everything in the physical world is made out of atoms. Atoms are made out of energy. And energy is made out of consciousness." By not taking into account energy (really Light-Energy, or Spirit-Power, or *Shakti*) as the connecting intermediary link between Consciousness and the physical world, their theses are rendered reductive and disintegral, on top of the other faults that sully them.

Loy also fails to consider the Buddhist Trikaya, *which is central to your hermeneutical Buddhist writings.*

It's disappointing, because sans *Trikayan* (or Trinitarian) metaphysics, Buddhist nonduality cannot be comprehensively elaborated. So Loy is not only guilty of ignoring Kashmir Shaivism, but also Dzogchen. Anyone who reads my Buddhism books [*Zen Mind, Thinker's Mind and Radical Dzogchen*] and compares them to Loy's will recognize a distinct difference in the level of Dharma elaboration and exegesis. In our current series of discussions on nonduality, I've focused on Kashmir Shaivism rather than Dzogchen because its system (unlike Dzogchen's, which is polluted by Madhyamaka nonsense) most closely coheres with my emanational/creational Mind-Only paradigm. But for a Buddhist writer such as Loy to discourse on nonduality without accounting for the *Trikaya* is nothing short of a black mark on his work.

CHAPTER FIFTEEN

Top-Down Monistic Idealism/ Bottom-Up Dualistic Realism

Okay, this is the last of our discussions on nonduality and Mind-Only metaphysics, so you should summarize your view and how it differs from others.

My view, in a nutshell, can be classified as "top-down monistic idealism/bottom-up dualistic realism." I contend that universal, timeless, spaceless Mind (or Consciousness), the Real, has become everything, the totality of space-time existents, which all are (phenomenally) real, because nothing unreal can come from the Real. In other words, whatever exists is real, but the ontological status of existents differs and must be hierarchically distinguished.

In accordance with Kashmir Shaivism (KS), I hold that once *Siva* (Mind, or Consciousness), via its inseparable *Shakti*, rolls out the universe of phenomenal existents, then duality—meaning separate space-time entities and consequent subject-object relations—ensues, and this manifest, dualistic reality is real, not an illusion.

So, as you've said before, from the top-down perspective, Consciousness, as the Progenitor, has primacy over existence, but once Siva, *for Divine sport, enacts (and hides Himself in)* Maya, *then existence has primacy over consciousness, which has been contracted into subject-object duality. And this explains why you can "marry" Kashmir Shaivism with Ayn*

Rand's Objectivism, because while KS explains uncreated, nondualistic Reality from the top down, Objectivism "completes it" by explaining created dualistic reality from the bottom up.

Very good. But I do want to make it clear that although I deeply resonate with both Kashmir Shaivism and Objectivism and freely integrate their philosophies with my own, I do not agree with every aspect of their teachings. Likewise, people can freely integrate aspects of my philosophy with their own, while not necessarily agreeing with everything I write or teach. In fact, I encourage this type of discriminating integration.

But Rand was an atheistic anti-mystic, which flies in the face of your God-oriented mysticism.

My view regarding Rand is the same as my view regarding Adi Da Samraj (whom I also receive flak for liking and "milking"): Don't throw the baby out with the bath water. Despite my major differences with aspects of their teachings (and behavior), I confess that I could not have "cracked the code" of the Enlightenment project sans their influence. As Ken Wilber puts it, "Even if Einstein was a complete psychotic, E still equals mc2."

In addition to your unique top-down/bottom-up perspective on nonduality and Mind-Only, what stands out in your paradigm is your integration of Kashmir Shaivism's 36-tattva schema and Kabbalah's Sefirotic Tree of Life as explanatory links that connect the "top" (the Divine Realm of Mind) with the "bottom" (the world).

Yes. Although I plan to further develop my descriptions of these links, I think that what I've provided in our talks provides a solid basis for theosophically explaining the hierarchical descent of Mind (or Consciousness) as Spirit (or Light-Energy) into matter (the world).

Deism, Monotheism, Pantheism, and Panentheism

What can you say about the pertinent "isms" of theism (deism, mono-theism, pantheism, and panentheism) in relation to your paradigm?

I'll summarize what I perceive each of these "isms" to mean, then answer your question.

Deism: This "ism" supports the existence of a creator God, but rejects the idea that this God actively intervenes in the human world. Deism also rejects the ideas of Divine revelation, the Holy Spirit, and the Trinity, and even the idea that holy books contain the Word of God.

Monotheism: Because theism can mean many gods or deities, it is only monotheism (meaning one God) that pertains to a monistic paradigm. Monotheism, exemplified by Christianity, Judaism, and Islam, holds that there is one Supreme Being/Creator God, distinct from His creation, who oversees and intervenes in human events. This God sustains a personal relation with His creatures.

Pantheism: The term "pantheism" derives from the Greek root *pan* (all) and *theos* (God). It means that the all, the cosmos, is identical with God, that Creator and creation (the universe) are not distinct from each other.

Panentheism: This term derives from *pan* (all) en (in) *theos* (God). Hence, it means that all (the universe) is in God, and God is in all. In other words, God transcends the world, but is immanent in it.

Millions of words have been written on each of these "isms" (not to mention their interrelatedness, or lack thereof); so my summary is hardly the final or full word on their respective meanings. That said, it should be clear that my paradigm most closely aligns with panentheism, which is compatible with top-down monistic idealism/bottom-up dualistic realism.

Would you classify your top-down monistic idealism / bottom-up dualistic realism paradigm as qualified nondualism?

Yes, it is similar to Vishishtadvaita Vedanta and other traditions that teach that God, or Mind, alone exists, while acknowledging the distinct reality of individual beings and the material world. Such traditions fall under the category of "qualified nondualism," or "qualified monism." My paradigm, however, is sui generis in that it provides a seminal "bridge," or intermundia, between the unmanifest Absolute and the manifest world we humans inhabit.

Awakening to the Nondual Holy One

Although God (or Mind) is immanent in all creatures as Self (or Buddha, or Christ), only man, on planet Earth, was created in "the image of God" and can consciously reflect the Deity. The Soul of man is a far cry from the shit he excretes and flushes down the toilet; so ontological distinctions regarding existents in the world must include their respective capacity to channel or express the Transcendent, the Holy. This, of course, implies dualism, and as I repeatedly make clear, top-down nonduality, meaning a single Mind (or Being-Consciousness) from whence all things stem, is compatible with bottom-up dualism, meaning separate, hierarchically distinct space-time existents, which appear, abide, and disappear in the timeless, spaceless "space" of Mind.

How do you define "Holy"?

Only the Godhead, the Trinity (or *Trikaya*)—timeless, spaceless, unborn, immaculate Consciousness-Energy—is Holy. When we speak of It as transcendent, It is Father; when we speak of It as immanent, It is Son; and when we refer to It as Energy (which links the Father and the Son), It is Spirit. The Holy One, the Godhead, is in the world, but not of it. The Holy One is ever nondual because His "three dimensions" (Father / *Dharmakaya*,

Son/*Buddha*, Spirit/*Sambhogakaya*) are intradivine; hence there is no dualistic "other" in the Godhead, but simply the three principal aspects of the "three-in-one" Deity, or Mind.

Nothing manifest (or born) is Holy, because everything created is compounded and subject to decay. Created objects (such as temples, holy books, and divine artifacts) can allude to the Unmanifested, the Uncompounded, but they themselves, as temporary appearances in space-time, are not truly Sacred, or Holy.

So the Holy is nondual, while the non-Holy is dual.

Yes. Space-time existents, the non-Holy, arise in, and of, Mind, but are not Mind. They are phenomenally real, but not Ultimately Real (or Holy). Mind, as Light-Energy, or Spirit-Power, through the medium of *Maya*, manifests as the entire spectrum of stepped-down energies, life forms, and matter. Although nondual, unmanifest Mind, via its *Shakti*, has become everything, it has not become anything, never being implicated in its own dualistic manifestation.

So how can one realize the reality of what you're saying?

Three ways. First, theosophically, by comprehending the reality of intelligent design by an unmanifest Divine Mind that subsumes the manifest universe of existents, and by acknowledging the wisdom of countless mystics and yogis throughout history who attest to the Reality of this Mind. Second, yogically, by mystically apprehending/contemplating/channeling the Holy Spirit, experiencing at-one-ment with it, and radically intuiting the nondual Reality that transcends the dualistic phenomenal world. Third, Spirit-fully/gnoseologically, by receiving the full, culminating descent of Divine Power (Clear-Light-Energy from above) that severs one's Heart-knot, which yields integral Self-Realization and the direct seeing/knowing that everything which appears or exists is a temporary modification or permutation of the Light-Energy of Mind (the all-encompassing Supreme Being-Consciousness, or Holy One).

The first way is readily accessible to intelligent, clear-thinking individuals, such as the iconic quantum physicist Erwin Schrodinger (1887-1961), who said, "The total number of minds in the universe is one. In fact, consciousness is a singularity phasing within all beings." To such individuals, it is apparent that a single Divine Mind is the Matrix from which both manifest existence and individual consciousness derive.

The second way is accessible to individuals who have been baptized by, and regularly abide in, the Holy Spirit, Divine *Shakti* from on high. Abidance in the Holy Spirit, the true Power of Now, which is Clear-Light Energy, bestows one with mystical gnosis of Mind as an all-subsuming, radiant Force-Flow.

The third way is accessible only to the rarest of beings, *mahasiddhas* (spiritually perfected adepts), who, by virtue of having cut the spiritual Heart-knot (felt-experienced two digits to the right of center of one's chest), unbrokenly rest in the Clear-Light Energy that is ceaselessly absorbed into and emitted from their now open Heart-center. For these beings, it is obvious that everything is a temporary modification or permutation of the timeless Light-Energy of God (or Mind).

How can one become baptized by the Holy Spirit, the Power of Now, and begin to experience Mind as an all-subsuming, radiant Force-Flow?

By practicing Power-of-Now meditation/contemplation (true Holy Communion). The book—*Nonduality and Mind-Only through the Prism of Reality*—that will result from our current series of discussions will contain a final chapter [Sixteen] that details this method.

CHAPTER SIXTEEN

Power-of-Now Meditation
(Holy Communion)

The idea of living in the Now and awakening to its Power was popularized by Eckhart Tolle—but until I began to write on the subject, beginning with my first book, *Beyond the Power of Now: A Guide to, and Beyond, Eckhart Tolle's Teachings* (published in 2012)—no one, including Eckhart Tolle, explained, in technical detail, how to live in the Now and channel its Power, or Light-Energy.

Unlike Eckhart Tolle, a fogged-out pop guru, I am an authority on the Power of Now, which, unbeknownst to Tolle, is a synonym for the Holy Spirit and yogic *Shakti*. Moreover, the Now is not the present moment (as Tolle would have you believe), but the timeless Supreme Source and Presence, which is Mind (or Consciousness).

In this chapter, I provide Power-of-Now Meditation (a.k.a. Holy, or Divine, Communion) Instructions (excerpted from my book *Electrical Christianity*) that explain how to access the timeless Now (or Divine Presence) and receive (or conduct) its en-Light-ening Energy (or divinizing Power), and thereby experience the Spirit-full Reality of Mind-Only nonduality. I also provide excerpts—"The Practice of True Holy Communion," "Ohm's Law and Spiritual Energy," and "Ohm's Law and the Eucharist"—from *Electrical Christianity* which, through the application of Ohm's Law and Hegelian dialectic, explain the "mechanics" of en-Light-enment.

Following the excerpts from *Electrical Christianity* is the section "Writings on Divine (Power-of-Now) Meditation," which consists of Kabbalah, Kashmir Shaivism, and Ramana Maharshi writings that provide further light on Divine (or Holy) Communion and Divine (Power-of-Now) reception. For more exhaustive and nuanced descriptions of Power-of-Now-type meditation/contemplation, refer to *Electrical Christianity* and my book *Radical Dzogchen*, which provides a ground-breaking Buddhist perspective on the En-Light-enment project.

Power-of-Now Meditation Instructions

Experiment with these instructions and use the ones that best enable you to plug into the Divine Presence, the Now, and pull down Divine Power, the Power of Now. Although I have numbered the recommendations, be advised that they overlap and intertwine and do not have to be practiced in the order in which I present them:

1) Sit upright, but relaxed, on a chair, bench, or meditation cushion.

2) Establish what the Buddha called "self-possession." In other words, feel yourself as the whole body, and then be consciously present as the whole body, the whole psycho-physical being. Randomly focusing your attention on your third-eye area and hands will enable you to coincide with your body, and thereby heal the body-mind split. When you consciously inhabit your whole body—and are wholly, or integrally, present to the whole (the totality of existence)—you are in proper position to receive and conduct the Power of Now, the Force-Flow from above.

3) "Gaze" into empty space. If you are "self-possessed," this "gaze" will amount to being whole-bodily present to (or in direct relationship to) the void. As soon as you become aware that you have retracted from your "position" of conscious connectedness to (or single-pointed focus on) the void, simply reassume, or attempt to reassume, your "stance" of holistic at-one-ment. To this end, you can randomly use an enquiry (such as "Avoiding relationship?") to instigate your resumption of communion with the void. When the void begins to "shine," it is experienced as Divine Presence. When the Power of the Presence pours down upon you, then "emptiness" has morphed into Spirit, and your "gaze into space" has transmuted into empowered Divine Communion.

4) Randomly focus your attention on your breath by being in direct relationship to your breathing cycle. When the breath "comes alive" as *prana-shakti*, or palpable intensified life-energy, simply remain present to it. Your communion with the breath cycle will transmute into true, or infused, Divine Communion when the *prana-shakti* morphs into Divine Power—the great *Shakti*, or Holy Spirit, poured down from above.

5) Totally relax your body (including your head) and utterly let go of your mind. Once you can connect to the *Shakti*, you will directly experience that letting go intensifies the Force-flow (or pressure) of the Spirit-current. Be an empty cup, ready to be filled with Divine Elixir from above. When you experience the Benediction, the Divine downpour, remain motivelessly present to it. Your searchless beholding of the *Shakti* will enable you to spontaneously merge with it.

These technical meditation instructions are all about facilitating communion, and then union, with the Divine. It is up to you to test them out and determine how useful they are for your practice. The ones that enable you to connect to the Divine Presence and channel Divine Power are the ones you should employ.

The Practice of True Holy Communion

Mainstream Christian churches are guilty of an egregious sin: They do not teach their members how to commune with the Deity and receive His Blessing Power, the Holy Spirit. There can be no true religion, no real spirituality, without contact with and reception of God's Spirit-Power. This book [*Electrical Christianity*] provides clear-cut, in-depth instructions on how to directly "plug into" the Divine Being, the Holy One, and literally "pull down" His Power. Grace is *not* an abstract principle; it *is* the palpable experience of God's Spirit-Power—and anyone who religiously (or devotedly and intensely) practices the discipline of true Holy (or Divine) Communion that I present in this book can experience the descent of Divine Power, the Holy Spirit.

The *true* Eucharist, the practice of Holy Communion (which, in its "awakened" form implies reception of the Holy Spirit), is the very heart of mystical Christianity—and I maintain that it is the foremost method for attaining salvation (spiritual en-Light-enment). Furthermore, if the practice of Holy Communion is augmented with an understanding of Electrical Christianity (Ohm's Law applied to Christianity), it becomes an even more potent en-Light-enment tool. Disciples of the Truth who meditate on the parallels between the Eucharist and Ohm's Law are sure to increase their understanding of spiritual life and improve their spiritual practice.

Ohm's Law and Spiritual Energy

Ohm's Law, the mathematical equation or formula for an electrical circuit, was discovered in 1827 and is the key to understanding the relationship between electrical and spiritual energy. Although I briefly touch upon other aspects of electricity, the central focus of my thesis is the correlation between Ohm's Law and spirituality. I can't prove that Ohm's Law holds true for spiritual energy, but even if it doesn't perfectly correlate with the spiritual process, it still stands out as an unparalleled formula and an ideal metaphor for explaining the spiritual-energetic phenomena—Holy Baptism, Holy Spirit reception, and divinization (whole-bodily en-Light-enment)—that spontaneously accompany the foundational practice of true Christianity: the Eucharist, or Holy Communion.

This Ohm's Law-Eucharist correlation, which I call the "Electrical Spiritual Paradigm (ESP)," equates Holy (or Divine) Communion with "plugged-in presence," reception of the Holy Spirit with "pulled-down power," and self-surrender with "perfect poverty." In electrical terms, plugged-in presence is *voltage*, pulled-down power is *amperage*, and perfect poverty is *ohms* (relative absence of resistance). If this seems intimidating, ungraspable or too abstract, relax; it will all become clear as you continue through the book, which explains the analogy from multiple perspectives. Once you grasp the Electrical Spiritual Paradigm, you'll marvel at its simplicity and elegance. More importantly, you'll understand—from a scientific-energetic perspective—how to connect to the Divine and channel its electrical-like Power, the Holy Spirit.

The great thing about Ohm's Law and spiritual energy is that you don't have to wait for science to prove they correlate; you can prove it to yourself in your own "laboratory," your own bodymind. And based on my own spiritual experience, Ohm's Law (or a modified version of it) does indeed hold true relative to genuine Christian spirituality. Moreover, once a disciple *spiritually* realizes, or conducts and feels, the electrical-like nature of Spirit-energy, he can use this realization as a springboard to radically intuiting, and perhaps ultimately achieving, the *summum bonum* of human existence: God-Realization, eternal abidance in Heaven, the Divine Domain.

Ohm's Law and the Eucharist

The dialectical spiritual practice you're describing does seem to mirror an electrical circuit, with the Spirit-current representing the amperage-like resolution of voltage-like conscious force and ohms-like reduced resistance. But how can you be sure that Ohm's Law applies to spirituality?

No one can prove (or disprove) that Ohm's Law applies to Spirit-conductivity. But based on my own spiritual experiences, it is obvious to me that Ohm's Law, or some approximate variation of it, applies to Eucharistic spirituality. Consequently, even if Ohm's Law does not exactly hold true for the practice of Holy Spirit communion and conductivity, it still provides a nonpareil metaphor for understanding the mechanics of the Eucharist.

For those of you unfamiliar with Ohm's Law, it states that "the strength or intensity of an unvarying electric current is directly proportional to the electromotive force and inversely proportional to the resistance in a circuit." Ohm's Law—where V = voltage (electromotive force), I = amperage (intensity of current), and R = ohms (units of resistance)—can be summarized in three formulas:

$$V = IR \;\; ; \;\; I = \frac{V}{R} \;\; ; \;\; R = \frac{V}{I}$$

(Note: Any form of the Ohm's Law equation can be derived from the other two via simple algebra.)

Translating Ohm's Law into a Eucharistic formula is simple. All we have to do is substitute communion, or connected consciousness (or consciousness-force), for voltage; spiritual energy (or intensity of the Spirit-current) for amperage; and ego-resistance (or degree of resistance to the Spirit-current) for ohms. Therefore, the Electrical Eucharistic formula— where C = communion, or connected consciousness (or consciousness-force); I = spiritual energy (or intensity of the Spirit-current); and R = ego-resistance (or degree of resistance to the Spirit-current)—can, like Ohm's Law, be summarized in three formulas:

$$C = IR \;\; ; \;\; I = \frac{C}{R} \;\; ; \;\; R = \frac{C}{I}$$

(Note: As with Ohm's Law, any of these equations can be derived from the other two via simple algebra.)

Can you simplify and summarize the Ohm's Law/Eucharist analogy?

Yes. The Holy Spirit is the electric current (amperage); Holy Communion is the electromotive force (voltage); and ego-resistance is the resistance to the flow of the current (ohms). Ohm's Law applied to Eucharistic spirituality tells us that the intensity of the Holy Spirit-current is directly proportional to one's Holy Communal (or relational) force and inversely proportional to one's ego-resistance to the inflowing Holy Spirit-current. Once you've been baptized by the Holy Spirit, you'll be able to palpably and viscerally experience the seeming reality of Ohm's Law in Eucharistic spirituality.

Writings on Divine (Power-of-Now) Meditation

DIALECTICAL KABBALISTIC MEDITATION

[This is an article I wrote that will be included in my forth-coming Kabbalah book.]

What's common to all proper descriptions of mystical med-itation, including those in Kabbalah, is an activistic approach (thesis) immediately followed by a passive state (antithesis). The synthesis that results (through the medium of the influx of the Holy Spirit) is Divine Union. In his fine text *Kabbalah: New Perspectives*, author Moshe Idel's descriptions of the mystical path allude to this dialectic. For example, he writes:

> Although the ecstatic Kabbalah emphasized an activistic approach to the mystical experience through its prescrip-tion of the mystical techniques, at the very moment of the experience, this activism was obliterated and replaced by a passive state.

Elsewhere he writes:

> Devekut [cleaving to God] is here closely related to the state of poverty or 'death'; indeed cleaving leads to the next mystical stage of total disengagement from the world. We can formulate a three-stage mystical path hinted at by R. Levi Isaac: (1) detachment from one's corporeal needs, (2) attaching of one's thought to God, and (3) spiritual 'poverty' or 'death' at the culmination of the mystical path. Like the annihilation that comes after union in the text of the Great Maggid, his disciple assumes a spiritual death that crowns one's experience of union.

Although the mystical dialectical synthesis in this quote is only described as union, the cognoscenti understand that this union is precipitated by reception of the Divine Efflux downward (into the Sacred Heart-center). Although R. Levi Isaac hints at a three-stage path, the first stage is not really a practice but the detached mindset that precedes the dialectical practices of attaching to God (via communion with His presence) and "poverty" (utter self-emptying or letting go).

Most people associate Kabbalah with the ten Sefirot and the Tree of Life, but that Kabbalah, which Idel terms the "theosophical Kabbalah," is the "lower Kabbalah." The "higher Kabbalah" is the "mystical Kabbalah," which focuses on the dialectical meditative practice of attaining union with God.

KABBALAH: NEW PERSPECTIVES

[This is an excerpt from the book *Kabbalah: New Perspectives* by Moshe Idel.]

"According to another treatise on [famous Kabbalist R. Hayyim] Vital, when the source of the highest human souls is blessed by the supernal influx, then it expands and draws a 'prophetic power' upon its soul so that he will understand and comprehend the secrets of the Torah. The greater this supernal influx, claims Vital, the greater is the human capability to understand the secrets of the Torah as if by the divine secret. This is an explicit reference to the crucial role of the pneuma for fathoming the Kabbalistic secrets concealed in the Torah."

SHAKTIPAT YOGA = POWER-OF-NOW MEDITATION

[This is an article I wrote that will be included in my forthcoming book *The Power of Now Meditation Guide*.]

Shaktipat (or *Saktipata*) is the Sanskrit term for the descent of Divine Power, or Grace (*Anugraha*). This Divine Power is the Power of Now, the Holy Spirit. The goal of Power-of-Now Meditation is the same as that of *Shaktipat* Yoga: to receive a progressively greater, or more intense, down-flow of Divine Power, to the degree that one's consciousness unites with it, thereby "producing," or unveiling, a State of nondual, or integral, Consciousness-Power, termed *Siva-Shakti* in the Indic tantric traditions.

In Kashmir Shaivism, the foremost Indic tantric tradition, there are six levels of Grace that a yogi can experience:

1) Supreme Supreme Grace

2) Supreme Medium Grace

3) Supreme Inferior Grace

4) Medium Supreme Grace

5) Medium Inferior Grace

6) Inferior Grace

The highest level of Grace, Supreme Supreme Grace, bestows the transcendence of duality, as one's individual soul, or consciousness, contracted *Siva*, unites with universal *Shakti*, resulting in the de-contraction of one's consciousness and the recognition of one's True Nature as *Siva-Shakti*, or Consciousness-Power. The second highest level of Grace, Supreme Medium Grace, confers intuition of this Divine Union, as one's consciousness experiences periodic merging with the down-poured *Shakti*. The levels of Grace below Supreme Medium Grace pertain to spirituality that doesn't involve the immediate apprehension and reception of Spirit-Power, or *Shakti*.

THE TRIADIC HEART OF SIVA

[This is an excerpt from the book *The Triadic Heart of Siva* by Paul Muller-Ortega.]

"Given the centrality, indeed, the crucial and indispensable nature of the process of recognition to the attainment of enlightenment, the question may arise: how precisely does it come about? What triggers the powerful experience of recognition? Most of the time, recognition arises from the liberating *saktipata* [*Shaktipat*], the descent of spiritual energy from *Siva*."

PRATYABHIJNAHRDAYAM: THE SECRET OF SELF-RECOGNITION

[This is an excerpt from the book *Pratyabhijnahrdayam: The Secret of Self-Recognition* by Jaideva Singh.]

"When, O mother, men renounce all mental activities and are poised in a pure state, being free from the bondage of the pursuit of sense-activities, then by thy grace is that supreme state realized at once, which rains down the nectar of undiminished and unparalleled happiness."

TALKS WITH SRI RAMANA MAHARSHI

[This is an excerpt from the book *Talks with Sri Ramana Maharshi* by Sri Munagala Venkataramiah.]

"*Malaparapaka*, *karmasamya*, and *saktipata* mean the same thing. A man is running the course of his *samskaras*; when taught that he is the Self, the teaching affects his mind and imagination runs riot. He feels helpless before the onrushing power. His experiences are only according to his imagination of the state "I am the Self," whatever he may conceive it to be. *Saktipata* alone confers the true and right experience."

Glossary

BUDDHIST/HINDU TERMS

Adi Buddha: The primordial *Buddha*, a.k.a. *Samantabhadra*, who is akin to *Siva* in tantric Shaivism.

Advaita: "Not two." Nonduality.

Advaita Vedanta: The nondual school of Hindu philosophy which asserts that one's True Self (*Atman*) is the same as the Divine Being (*Brahman*).

Akasha: The ether, or universal space element, wherefrom the four fundamental elements (fire, earth, air, water) derive.

Alaya: The unborn Realm, universal Mind.

Alaya-vijnana: The *Alaya* (universal Consciousness) conjoined with *manas* by *vijnana* in the Heart-center/cave, the *Tathagatagarbha*. A synonym for *citta*, which functions as the "storehouse consciousness," or repository, of one's psychical seed impressions/tendencies (*samskaras*).

Amrita Nadi: The Force (or *Shakti*)-current between the spiritual Heart-center and the crown. The terminal portion/branch of *Sushumna Nadi*, through which immortal "Nectar," Blessing/Blissing Clear-Light Energy, flows.

Anahata: The subtle-body heart *chakra*.

Anu: The (contracted) empirical individual as a point of awareness in the midst of Infinity.

Anugraha-Shakti: Divine Blessing Power, or Grace.

Asana: Psycho-physical "position," "seat," or "stance."

Atman: A synonym for Self, Christ, and *Buddha*. Immanent *Brahman*.

Bhagavan: A "Blessed One" or Divine personage. Etymologically, *Bhagavan* means penis in the vagina, signifying a being who has united *Siva* and *Shakti*, and thus realized the Self.

Bodhicitta: Enlightened, or Awakened, Consciousness. *Buddhahood*.

Bodhisattva: An Enlightenment-minded seeker of *Bodhicitta*.

Brahman: Ultimate Reality. The changeless, infinite Divine Being, typically described as *Sat-Cit-Ananda*.

Buddha/Buddha-Nature: A synonym for *Atman*, Self, or Christ. The immanent *Dharmakaya*, or Mind.

Buddhadharma: Buddhist *Dharma*, or Teaching.

Buddhahood: *Bodhicitta*, or *Nirvana*.

Buddhi: The intellect, or discriminating intelligence of the mind. Sometimes referred to as the "higher mind," in contrast to *manas*, the "lower mind."

Chakra/Cakra: Literally a "wheel" or "center." The major *chakras* are subtle-body centers where *pranic* channels converge into rotating vortices of energy, which, when blocked, can be likened to "knots," and when open, can produce various "spiritual" phenomena.

Cit: Universal, transcendental Consciousness.

Citta: Immanent Consciousness itself (*Cit*) intertwined with *manas* and contracted by grasping (or acts of binding attention) engendered by *vijnana*. When *citta* is permanently de-contracted, it shines as *Cit*, or *Bodhicitta,* and though functioning as *manas* and *vijnana*, it is no longer contracted by them. This is tantamount to the conversion of the *Alaya-vijnana* from an "organ" of bondage and becoming to an "instrument" of Enlightenment.

Cittamatra: A subsystem of *Yogacara* which asserts that a single universal Mind (or Consciousness) has become everything. As such, it is akin to Hindu Kashmir Shaivism and Tibetan *Dzogchen*, which likewise assert that a single omnipresent Consciousness or Awareness (*Siva* or *Dharmakaya*), has manifested as all existents.

Citi: Consciousness-Power.

Darshan: The auspicious seeing/beholding of a holy person or object.

Dharma/*dharma*: When capitalized, spiritual teaching or Truth or Law. When uncapitalized, a conditional thing. Also one's right "duty," or karmic "role."

Dharmadhatu: The *Dharmakaya* as the all-pervading, spaceless Substratum underlying phenomenal existence.

Dharmakaya: Universal, timeless Awareness or Consciousness.

Dharmamegha: The "rained-down" descent of the *Dharmakaya* (as the *Sambhogakaya*) which, when "full-blown," "produces" *Bodhicitta*. Sometimes, the term "Great *Dharmamegha*" is used to differentiate "full-blown" *Dharmamegha* from "partial" *Dharmamegha*.

Dzogchen: The Great Perfection. The Tibetan Buddhist and Bon traditions/practices aimed at directly realizing the primordial State of Being.

Guru: Remover of darkness, or ignorance. A Self-realized being who unobstructedly radiates Light.

Hridayam: The spiritual Heart. A synonym for the immanent Self and its Center, relative to the body, through which it radiates.

Kaivalya: Isolation, meaning exclusive realization of, or absorption in, the Self, or *Buddha*, sans defiling taints.

Kosha: Sheath, or covering.

Kundalini: The "serpent power." The dynamic force-flow of "uncoiled" energy that accompanies spiritual awakening. The so-called "higher *Kundalini*" refers to *Shaktipat*, the descent of Divine Power.

Madhyamaka: A school of Mahayana Buddhism, systematized by Nagarjuna, which emphasizes the emptiness of all phenomena.

Mahamudra: The Great Seal, Symbol, and Gesture. And the "Great Gesture," or yogic "Holo-Act," is uniting the son light (the *nirmanakaya*) with the Mother Light (the *Sambhogakaya*), which yields realization of the Father (the *Dharmakaya*).

Mahasiddha: A spiritually perfected adept, who, by virtue of having cut the spiritual Heart-knot (felt-experienced two digits to the right of center of one's chest), unbrokenly rests in the Clear-Light Energy that is ceaselessly absorbed into and emitted from his Heart-center (*Hridayam*).

Mala: Defilement that obstructs Enlightenment.

Manas: The mind that processes and mediates sensory information and habit-tendencies (*vasanas*). The mind in general.

Maya: That which has been "measured out" from the Immeasurable. Phenomenal existence or reality.

Maya-Shakti: The contracting/cloaking/measuring/dividing power of *Siva* (the Supreme Being-Consciousness).

Moksha: Liberation.

Nadis: Energy channels in the body. These include the subtle-body channels through which *prana* and *kundalini* flow and, in the case of *Amrita Nadi*, the causal-body channel through which immortal "Nectar," Blessing/Blissing Clear-Light Energy, streams.

Nirmanakaya: The immanent *Dharmakaya*. The Enlightened form body, or manifest *Buddha*. Akin to the Christian Son, or Christ.

Nirvana: The end of becoming (*samsara*), which signifies Blissful (Divine) Being. Equivalent to Hindu *Sat-Cit-Ananda*.

Prakriti: The primal "matter" or substance from which the physical and mental universe evolves. Whatever is created is *prakritic* in nature, meaning finite, conditioned, and temporary.

Prana: Etheric life-force; equivalent to *chi*.

Prana-Shakti: Etheric life-force energy.

Pranayama: Conscious breathing exercise(s) aimed at balancing and/or intensifying the flow of *prana* through one's subtle-body *nadis*.

Purusa: In Kashmir Shaivism, the empirical limited/conditioned self. In Samkhya and the *Yoga Sutras*, the Self, immanent pure Consciousness.

Sadhana: Spiritual practice.

Samantabhadra: The primordial *Buddha*, a.k.a. *Adi-Buddha*, who is akin to *Siva* in tantric Shaivism.

Sambhogakaya: The Bliss, or Light, Body. The *Dharmakaya* as Blessing/Blissing Clear-Light Energy. Equivalent to Hindu *Shakti* and the Christian Holy Spirit/Ghost.

Samsara: The cycle of birth and death. "Becoming," the succession of limited and unsatisfactory states of being.

Samsarin: A being subject to *samsara*.

Samskaras: Subconscious psychical impressions in the *citta*, or *Alaya-vijnana*, which, when activated, concatenate into *vasanas,* desire-impulses, or habit-energies.

Sankoca: Contraction

Sat: Being

Sat-Cit-Ananda: Being-Consciousness-Bliss.

Shakti (Sakti): Divine Power, or Clear-Light Energy. Equivalent to the Buddhist *Sambhogakaya* and the Christian Holy Spirit.

Shaktipat (Saktipata): The descent of Divine Power (or Grace), which can occur spontaneously in a disciple or be instigated by a spiritual master.

Siddha: A "Completed One." Equivalent to a *Buddha* or Enlightened Master.

Siddhi: Paranormal power possessed by a yogi or *Siddha*.

Siva: The personification of the Absolute in Hindu Shaivism. Akin to the *Adi-Buddha*, or *Samantabhadra*, in Vajrayana Buddhism.

Siva-Shakti: The Absolute (or Divine Being) depicted as Consciousness-Power rather than just Consciousness (*Siva*).

Soma: Ambrosial Light-Energy; Divine Elixir.

Sushumna: One of the three principal *nadis* that connect the base of the spine to the crown. As the so-called central channel, it lies between the so-called left channel, *ida*, and the so-called right channel, *pingala*, each of which coil around it and intersect at points within it, forming the major "spinal" *chakras*.

Sutra / Sutta: "Thread" or scripture.

Tantra: Derives from "tan," which means to weave and expand. A tantric yogi weaves the strands of his nature into a unified whole, which frees and "expands" (or de-contracts) his consciousness. Spiritual alchemy: the transubstantiation of one's entire being into single, radiant Intensity.

Tathagata: A *Buddha*, a "thus-gone-one" who abides eternally (or timelessly) in *Nirvana*.

Tathagatagarbha: The "womb" or matrix where a *Buddha*, or "thus-gone one," is "reborn," or Awakened. Akin to the "cave of the Heart" in Hindu yoga.

Tattva: Ontological principle or category.

Tattvas (per Kashmir Shaivism): (1) *Siva*: The Supreme Being-Consciousness; (2) *Shakti*: *Siva* as Divine Power; (3)

Sadasiva: Siva as Divine Will (*Iccha-Shakti*); (4) *Isvara: Siva*
as Divine "Mastermind" (*Jnana-Shakti*); (5) *Sadvidya: Siva*
as Divine "Creatrix" (*Kriya-Shakti*); (6) *Maya*: phenomenal reality, "measured out" by the "Immeasurable One,"
Siva; (7-11) The five *Kancukas* (coverings), the root veils
of *Maya: Kala*: contracted/cloaked Power/Sovereignty
of *Siva*; *Vidya*: contracted/cloaked Omniscience of *Siva*;
Raga: contracted/cloaked Bliss of *Siva*; *Kaala*: contracted/
cloaked Timelessness of *Siva*; *Nityati*: contracted/cloaked
Spacelessness of *Siva*; (12) *Purusa*: the empirical limited/
conditioned person/experient; (13) *Prakriti*: the objective
material (gross and subtle) manifestation experienced by
an individual *Purusa*; (14) *Buddhi*: the discriminating intelligence of the mind; the so-called "higher mind"; (15) *Ahamkara*: the separate-self sense, contracted I-Consciousness;
(16) *Manas*: the mind that processes and mediates sensory
information and habit-tendencies; the so-called "lower
mind"; (17-21) *Jnanendriyas* or *Buddhindriyas*: the "five
powers of sense-perception": smelling (*ghranendriya*), tasting (*rasanendriya*), seeing (*caksurindriya*), feeling by touch
(*sparsanendriya*), hearing (*sravanendriya*); (22-26) *Karmendriyas*: the "five powers of action": speaking (*vagindriya*),
handling (*hastendriya*), locomotion (*padendriya*), excreting
(*payvindriya*), sexual action and restfulness (*upasthendriya*);
(27-31) *Tanmatras*: the "five primary elements of sense perception": sound-as-such (*sabda-tanmatra*), touch-as-such
(*sparsa-tanmatra*), color-as-such (*rupa-tanmatra*), flavor-as-
such (*rasa-tanmatra*), odor-as-such (*gandha-tanmatra*); (32-
36) *Mahabhutas*: the "five gross elements": space (*akasha*),
air (*vayu*), fire (*teja* or *agni*), water (*apas*), earth (*prthivi*).

Trikaya: The Buddhist Triple Body (*Dharmakaya, Sambhogakaya,
Nirmanakaya*). The *Dharmakaya* viewed three-dimensionally

as: transcendental, universal Consciousness; Blessing/ Blissing Clear-Light Energy; and immanent, embodied Consciousness.

Unmesa: The externalization of *Iccha-Shakti*; the start of the manifestation process via *Kriya-Shakti*.

Upaya: Means to Enlightenment.

Vasana: Habit-energy or desire-impulse.

Vijnana: This term has two meanings: 1) consciousness functioning as discriminating intelligence, the "higher mind," and 2) consciousness functioning dualistically, meaning at every level of mind.

Vijnaptimatra: The *Yogacara* "mind-only" school, which asserts that the world is nothing but ideas, with no Reality or realities behind them, and that all *dharmas* (or things) are mere mental projections, or cognitions, or representations, of one's individual mind.

Yogacara: The Mahayana Buddhist "Mind-Only" school, which consists of two distinct subschools: *Vijnaptimatra* (which asserts that all things are mere mental projections), and *Cittamatra* (which views all things as manifestations of universal Mind).

Zen: The term *Zen* (*Ch'an* in Chinese) derives from *dhyana* (Sanskrit), which means meditation. Hence, Zen Buddhism is Buddhism which emphasizes meditation, while deemphasizing other aspects of *Buddhadharma*.

KABBALAH TERMS

Adam Kadmon: The personification of the Absolute. As such, an analogue for Shaivism's *Siva*, the Divine personification of Being-Consciousness, the One Mind.

Ain: Per conventional Kabbalah, *Ain* mean nothingness. Per me, *Ain* means no-thing, not nothingness. It signifies God not as a thing, but as the unmanifest Divine Being (or "Thing"-in-Itself) from which all manifest things derive.

Ain Sof: Signifies God as endless and limitless.

Ain Sof Aur: Denotes God, the Divine Being (or Mind, or Consciousness), as limitless Light-Energy (or Spirit-Power); hence it is equivalent to *Siva-Shakti*—spaceless, timeless Consciousness-Energy.

Assiah: The fourth of the Four Worlds. It is the "World of Action," the physical world (or universe) of differentiated existents interacting in constant flux. At this "gross" level of existence, a.k.a. *Maya*, there is maximal concealment of the Divine, as the involutionary process is complete. Emanation, through the medium of the ether, has morphed into material creation; and embodied, ensouled beings living in this World must undergo an evolutionary process in order to free their imprisoned souls and regain their Divine status.

Atziluth: The first emanated world/dimension from *Ain Sof Aur*. It is considered "pure divinity," and as such, "near to God." It is also referred to as the "World of Causes," meaning God's Will to create the universe of existents, which functions under the law of cause and effect. *Atziluth* is an analogue for Kashmir Shaivism's *Sadasiva*, who is *Siva* as Divine Will (*Iccha,* or *Iccha-Shakti*), the Omnipotent One.

Binah: The (Saturn-like) Sefirah that pertains to worldly understanding, the binding "lower mind," as opposed to the "other-worldly," or spiritual, Understanding/Wisdom of *Chokmah*, the unbinding "higher mind."

Briah: The "World of Creation," the second emanated dimension from *Ain Sof Aur*. It is an analogue for Plato's "World of Forms" and Kashmir Shaivism's *Isvara* (*Jnana*, or *Jnana-Shakti*), the Omniscient One, who "Masterminds" the creative descent of *Ain Sof Aur*, or *Siva-Shakti*, into the third world, *Yetzirah*, the ether. *Briah* is the domain of "pure intellect," meaning God, or Mind (prior to the emergence of space and time), "imagining," and thus "creating," the archetypal forms that will begin to "take shape" in the ether, the primordial space element.

Chesed: The (Jupiter-like) Sefirah that represents benevolent, generous energy, and also the "wheel of fortune," meaning the speculative, unpredictable nature of life.

Chokmah: The (Uranus-like) Sefirah that represents the "higher mind," or Wisdom. It correlates with the *buddhi* (discriminating intelligence in Yoga philosophy), and as such, is about detaching from the binding mind-forms of discursive thinking.

Da'at: The (Neptune-like) so-called "invisible" Sefirah, because until the mystic, or Kabbalist, is "initiated" (Spirit-baptized), and receives *Siva* as *Shakti* (the Holy Spirit), he cannot "see," or perceive, this Sefirah, which is like an ineffable empty cup that becomes noticeable only after it is filled with Elixir, or *Soma*, from *Siva/Keter*. Once the empty cup, or Holy Chalice, is filled, *Da'at* (or "She") is revealed as the inseparable Divine Consort of *Keter/Siva* (or "He").

Four Worlds: The four primary dimensions of existence stemming from the Absolute, *Ain Sof Aur*. Whereas the Tree of Life pertains to our solar system, the Four Worlds are universal and describe the dimensional descent of *Ain Sof Aur* into emanation and creation. These four dimensions, in order, from highest to lowest, are: *Atziluth*, *Briah*, *Yetzirah*, and *Assiah*.

Gevurah: The masculine (Mars-like) Sefirah that represents "strength," or "might" and "severity."

Hod: The (Mercury-like) Sefirah that represents the conventional mind, which focuses on judgment, but which through true prayer can re-orient itself to receiving Divine Blessing Power, a.k.a. "Splendor" and "Glory."

Keter: The highest, or most holy, Sefirah on the Tree of Life, commonly described as "Crown." Keter represents Consciousness itself, the atomic human Soul, the *Atman*. *Keter* is an ideal match for Pluto, the "atomic" planet, which, in its highest expression, represents penetrating consciousness-force, or soul-power. The sage who cuts through spiritual materialism (all the "idols" of the mind), and unites his soul, or consciousness, with the Holy Spirit, epitomizes pure Plutonic power. Although *Keter* is placed at the crown of the Tree of Life, signifying its apex position in the Sefirotic hierarchy, in reality, it is ultimately the Heart of the Tree, shining as diamond-like Consciousness itself through the medium of *Tiferet*.

Netzach: The feminine (Venus-like) Sefirah *Netzach*, which is the counterpart to masculine (Mars-like) *Gevurah*, represents fertility and material growth; hence she refers to "victory or "success" on the earthly plane.

Partzufim: Sefirot reconfigured into structured, interrelated components (in the form of Archetype personas) that, putatively, restore universal harmony.

Ruach HaKodesh: The Holy Spirit as Divine Power; the "action" of the *Shekinah*.

Sefirot: The ten (or eleven) "nodes" or "spheres" that comprise the Kabbalistic Tree of Life. These Sefirah have been described as potencies, vessels, channels, intermediaries, instruments, hypostases, logoi, and more—but perhaps the most graphic description of them is as prisms. I say this because, as the cognoscenti know, the Sefirot are analogues for the planets (or planetary spheres) in our solar system (which, astrologically, include the Sun and the Moon), which function prismatically to channel a spectrum of energies particular to their own (Divinely designated) domains and agencies. The standard ten Sefirotic nodes, from top to bottom, are: *Keter*, *Chokmah*, *Binah*, *Chesed*, *Gevurah*, *Tiferet*, *Netzach*, *Hod*, *Yesod*, and *Malkhut*. The so-called eleventh Sefirah, *Da'at*, is invisible to non-mystics. Upon Spirit (or *Shakti*) "initiation," "confirmation," and "sanctuary," it is realized to be an inseparable component of *Keter*, thereby, in effect, forming *Keter-Da'at* as a single Sefirah, thus preserving the classic ten-Sefirot paradigm.

Shekinah: The Holy Spirit/Ghost as Divine Presence.

Shevirath Ha Kelim: The "shattering of the vessels (Sefirot)" in God's act of creation.

Tiferet: The Sefirah that corresponds with the soul/individual, who, through union with the Spirit, can shine as immanent, radiant Consciousness-Force, thereby transforming contracted *Tiferet*, the son, into En-Light-ened *Tiferet*, the Son.

Tikkun: The universal cosmos/harmony engendered by the putative restructuring of the Sefirot into *Partzufim*.

Tohu: The universal chaos caused by the "shattering of the vessels (Sefirot)" in God's act of creation.

Tsimtsum: The universal contraction of God (Being-Consciousness-Energy) in His act of creation.

Yesod: The (Moon-like) Sefirah that corresponds with subconscious emotions and feelings. Upon spiritual Awakening, it is the Feeling of Being, the reflective component of the Being-ness of Self, or Son, that shines through (Sun-like) *Tiferet*.

Yetzirah: The "World of Formation," the third of the four worlds/dimensions proceeding from *Ain Sof Aur*. The dimension of space wherein the four basic elements (fire, earth, air, and water) that compose the physical world emerge. Unbeknownst to modern science, space is not empty, but is the primal substance, or element, underlying the material world. The space element, the ether, or *Akasha*, gives rise to the four basic elements and the so-called "quantum activity" that precedes physical materialization.

Spiritual Reading List

Advaita Vedanta

<u>Highly Recommended</u>

Ashtavakra Gita, trans. Hari Prasad Shastri. (Timeless Advaita Vedanta text. Available at www.shantisadan.org. Other translations also available.)

Be As You Are: The Teachings of Ramana Maharshi, David Godman. (Best introductory book on the teachings of Ramana Maharshi.)

Sat-Darshana Bhashya and Talks with Maharshi, Sri Ramanasramam. (A learned devotee's in-depth consideration of Ramana Maharshi's teachings within the framework of Indian-yogic philosophy.)

Sri Ramana Gita, Ramana Maharshi. (An utterly unique, ultra-profound text that details the function of the *Amrita Nadi* in the Self-realization process.)

Talks with Sri Ramana Maharshi, Ramana Maharshi. (Must-reading. A truly great and inspiring book. Avoid the dumbed-down version published by Inner Directions.)

Sat-Darshana Bhashya, *Sri Ramana Gita*, and *Talks with Sri Ramana Maharshi* are available at www.arunachala.org.)

<u>Recommended</u>

Be Who You Are (or any of Jean Klein's books), Jean Klein.

I Am That: Talks with Sri Nisargadatta Maharaj, Maurice Frydman. (Classic, uber-popular text.)

Silence of the Heart, Robert Adams.

Vivekachudamani (Crest Jewel of Discrimination), trans. Swami Prabhavananda and Christopher Isherwood. (Other translations of Shankara's teachings also available.)

Who Am I? Meditation, Ramaji. (If you like this text, get his *The Spiritual Heart*.)

Buddhism (Original)

<u>Highly Recommended</u>

Some Sayings of the Buddha: According to the Pali Canon, F.L. Woodward. (Outstanding presentation of the Buddha's core teachings.)

The Living Thoughts of Gotama the Buddha, Ananda Coomaraswamy and I.B. Horner. (Classic text. Great presentation of what the Buddha really taught.)

The Wings to Awakening: An Anthology from the Pali Canon, Thanissaro Bhikku. (Outstanding translation of and commentary on the Buddha's essential meditation teachings. Free download available on the Internet.)

<u>Recommended</u>

Buddhism: An Outline of its Teachings and Schools, Hans Wolfgang Schuman. (Solid academic book.)

In the Buddha's Words: An Anthology of Discourses from the Pali Canon, Bhikku Bodhi. (Comprehensive introduction to the Buddha's teachings.)

Mindfulness in Plain English, Venerable Henepola Gunaratana. (Basic introductory text on insight meditation.)

The Doctrine of Awakening: The Attainment of Self-Mastery According to the Earliest Buddhist Texts, Julius Evola. (Unique consideration of Pali Buddhism.)

The Heart of Buddhist Meditation, Nyaponika Thera. (Classic text on insight meditation.)

The Way of Non-Attachment, Dhiravamsa. (Unique Krishnamurti-influenced book on insight meditation. Out of print.)

Buddhism (Tibetan)

<u>Highly Recommended</u>

Principal Yogacara Texts: Indo-Tibetan Sources of Dzogchen Mahamudra, Rodney P. Devenish. (Best Yogacara text I've encountered.)

Radical Dzogchen: The Direct Way to En-Light-enment, L. Ron Gardner. (Clearest and most demystifying teachings on Dzogchen practice and Dharma. Must-reading for Dzogchen students.)

Teachings of Tibetan Yoga, Garma C.C. Chang. (Superb Mahamudra presentation. Must-reading for serious meditators.)

The Cycle of Day and Night, Namkhai Norbu. (Outstanding Dzogchen meditation manual. Must-reading for serious meditators.)

The Golden Letters, John Myrdhin Reynolds. (Scholarly exposition of the history and practice of Dzogchen in relation to Garab Dorje, the first teacher of Dzogchen.)

The Precious Treasury of the Way of Abiding, Longchen Rabjam. (Marvelous ultra-mystical text by a revered Vajrayana master. If you appreciate this book, get *A Treasure Trove of Scriptural Transmission: A Commentary on The Precious Treasury of the Basic Space of Phenomena* by the same author. Other translations/annotations of Rabjam's texts are available.)

Recommended

Cutting Through Spiritual Materialism, Chogyam Trungpa. (Enlightening text by a modern "crazy wisdom" master.)

Naked Awareness, Karma Chagme. (Excellent material on Dzogchen and Mahamudra.)

Self-Liberation Though Seeing with Naked Awareness, John Myrdhin Reynolds. (Compare this translation of/commentary on Padmasambhava's *Yoga of Knowing the Mind and Seeing Reality* to W.Y. Evans-Wentz's in *The Tibetan Book of the Great Liberation*.)

The Supreme Source, Namkhai Norbu. (The fundamental tantric text of Dzogchen.)

The Tibetan Book of the Great Liberation, W.Y. Evans-Wentz. (Classic translation of/commentary on Padmasambhava's *Yoga of Knowing the Mind and Seeing Reality*. Compare this translation/commentary to John Myrdhin Reynolds's in *Self-Liberation Through Seeing with Naked Awareness*. Skip Carl Jung's ridiculous "Psychological Commentary.")

Tibetan Yoga and Secret Doctrines, W.Y. Evans-Wentz. (Classic, ultra-mystical text.)

Wonders of the Natural Mind, Tenzin Wangyal. (The essence of Dzogchen in the Native Bon Tradition of Tibet.)

(Although I have little good to say about Longchen Rabjam's *Precious Treasury of the Genuine Meaning*, it's must-reading for those interested in standard Dzogchen *togal*, as is Jigme Lingpa's *Yeshe Lama*, another text I hold in low regard. Sam van Schaik's *Approaching the Great Perfection: Simultaneous and Gradual Methods of Dzogchen Practice in the Longchen Nyingtig* and *Naked Seeing: The Great Perfection, the Wheel of Time and Visionary Buddhism in Renaissance Tibet* by Christopher Hatchell are interesting, information-packed academic texts that serious students of *togal* will appreciate.)

Buddhism (Zen)

<u>Highly Recommended</u>

The Diamond Sutra and the Sutra of Hui Neng, trans. A.F. Price. (Other translations of these timeless sutras also available.)

Tracing Back the Radiance: Chinul's Korean Way of Zen, Robert Buswell, Jr. (Outstanding account of a great Zen master's spiritual evolution.)

Zen Mind, Thinkers Mind: New Perspectives on Buddhadharma, Consciousness, and Awakening, L. Ron Gardner. (Easily the foremost text for "cracking the code" of Zen practice and philosophy. Must-reading.)

The Zen Teaching of Huang Po, John Blofeld. (Easily the best book on original Zen. Must-reading.)

<u>Recommended</u>

Kensho, The Heart of Zen, Thomas Cleary. (My favorite Cleary text on Zen.)

Practical Zen: Meditation and Beyond, Julian Daizan Skinner. (Excellent beginner-intermediate Zen instruction text.)

The Lankavatara Sutra, trans. D.T. Suzuki. (Avoid Red Pine's "butchered" *The Lankavatara Sutra: Translation and Commentary*.)

The Practice of Zen, Garma C.C. Chang. (Great autobiographical accounts of enlightenment. Out of print.)

The Rinzai Zen Way: A Guide to Practice, Meido Moore. (Excellent beginner-intermediate Zen instruction text.)

The Three Pillars of Zen, Philip Kapleau. (Classic, popular Rinzai Zen text that emphasizes the satori experience.)

The Way of Zen, Alan Watts. (Classic introductory text by the godfather of American Zen.)

Zen Mind, Beginner's Mind, Shunryu Suzuki. (Classic, ultra-popular Soto Zen text.)

Zen Teaching of Instantaneous Awakening, Ch'an Master Hui Hai; trans. John Blofeld. (Fine Dharma instructions by a great Chinese Ch'an master.)

(Scholarly types will enjoy Heinrich Dumoulin's *Zen Buddhism: A History (India and China)* and *Zen Buddhism: A History (Japan)*, Vol. 2. Serious students of Buddhist philosophy will appreciate Garma C.C. Chang's *The Buddhist Teaching of Totality*, which expounds Hwa Yen Buddhism's all-embracing philosophy in relation to Zen. If you enjoy reading Zen, check out Thomas Cleary's numerous books at Amazon.com. Edward Conze's *Selected Sayings from the Perfection of Wisdom* is a fine anthology of sayings from the Prajnaparamita Sutras, including the *Heart Sutra*.)

Christianity, Judaism, and Gnosticism

<u>Highly Recommended</u>

Electrical Christianity: A Revolutionary Guide to Jesus' Teachings and Spiritual Enlightenment, L. Ron Gardner. (Ground-breaking text that radically demystifies and explains Christian mysticism and en-Light-enment).

Meditations on the Tarot, Valentin Tomberg. (An astonishing journey into Christian Hermeticism. Must-reading for anyone interested in Christian mysticism.)

Meister Eckhart. (*The Complete Mystical Works of Meister Eckhart* is the book I recommend—but it costs $98. *Meister Eckhart*, trans. Raymond B. Blakney, is a fine compilation of Eckhart's sermons, and goes for about $30. Scholarly types will want to supplement either of the aforementioned books with *The Mystical Thought of Meister Eckhart* by Bernard McGinn.)

Mysticism, Evelyn Underwood. (Wonderful, classic, early twenti-eth-century text by the first lady of Christian mysticism.)

The Foundations of Mysticism, Bernard McGinn. (Extraordinary presenta-tion of the Western mystical tradition. Must-reading for scholarly types.)

Recommended

Inner Christianity, Richard Smoley. (Clear and thoughtful guide to the esoteric Christian tradition.)

Jesus Christ, Sun of God, David Fideler (Fascinating read on ancient cosmology, gnostic symbolism, Pythagorean number theory, and Hellenistic gematria.)

Jewish Meditation, Aryeh Kaplan.

Open Mind, Open Heart, Thomas Keating. (Classic, best-selling text on the Gospel's contemplative dimension.)

The Big Book of Christian Mysticism: The Essential Guide to Contemplative Spirituality, Carl McColman. (Good introductory text and resource guide for those interested in Christian mysticism.)

The Mystic Christ, Ethan Walker. (Excellent book for mainstream Christians.)

The Practice of the Presence of God, Brother Lawrence, Robert Edmondson, and Jonathon Wilson-Hartgrove. (Classic text on the practice of establishing a conscious relationship with the Divine.)

The Secret Book of John, trans. Stevan Davies.

The Sermon on the Mount According to Vedanta, Swami Prabhavananda.

The Way of a Pilgrim and the Pilgrim Continues His Way, Multiple fine translations available. (Inspiring book for practitioners of prayer and mantra meditation.)

(Scholarly types into Western Christian mysticism will love all the fine texts by Prof. Bernard McGinn. Check out his seven-volume The Presence of God Series, which begins with the highly recommended *The Foundations of Mysticism*. Beyond this series, McGinn has graced us with *The Essential Writings of Christian Mysticism*, an immensely rich anthology of the greatest Christian mystical literature. Selections in this volume include writings from such great mystics as Origen, Augustine, Pseudo-Dionysius the Areopagite, St. John of the Cross, Bernard of Clairvaux, Meister Eckhart, John Ruysbroeck, and many more. For a scholarly consideration of Jewish mysticism, I recommend Gershom Scholem's *Major Trends in Jewish Mysticism and Moshe Idel's Kabbalah: New Perspectives*. Scholem's text is the canonical modern work on the nature and history of Jewish mysticism, while Idel's is the foremost scholarly consideration of Kabbalah.)

Daism

Highly Recommended

Hridaya Rosary (Four Thorns of Heart-Instruction), Adi Da Samraj. (Excellent technical devotional-meditation book.)

The Knee of Listening, Adi Da Samraj. (Best spiritual autobiography ever written. Must-reading for mystics. Get a copy of the latest edition, but also get a copy of an earlier edition written under the name of Franklin Jones or Bubba Free John. These earlier editions, unlike later and current editions, contain Da's outstanding "Meditation of Understanding," instructions on the practice of "real meditation," or "radical understanding.")

The Liberator: The "Radical" Reality-Teachings of The Great Avataric Sage, Adi Da Samraj. Adi Da Samraj.

The Method of the Siddhas, Adi Da Samraj. (A truly great spiritual book. Out of print and only available used. Try to get a copy written under the name of Franklin Jones or Bubba Free John. The current revised edition of the book, entitled *My "Bright" Word*, lacks the direct visceral impact of the original text.)

The Pneumaton, Adi Da Samraj. (Ultra-esoteric consideration of "Pneuma," the Spirit.)

The Way of Perfect Knowledge: The "Radical" Practice of Transcendental Spirituality in the Way of Adidam. Adi Da Samraj.

Recommended

He-And-She Is Me: The Indivisibility of Consciousness and Light In the Divine Body of the Ruchira Avatar, Adi Da Samraj.

Ruchira Avatara Hridaya-Siddha Yoga:The Divine (and Not Merely Cosmic) Spiritual Baptism in the Way of Adidam, Adi Da Samraj.

Santosha Adidam: The Essential Summary of the Divine Way of Adidam, Adi Da Samraj.

The All-Completing and Final Divine Revelation to Mankind: A Summary Description Of The Supreme Yoga Of The Seventh Stage Of Life In The Divine Way Of Adidam, Adi Da Samraj.

(The four books on the Recommended List contain a number of the same essays. Nonetheless, each book includes enough unique material to merit its reading.)

Hinduism (Yoga)

Highly Recommended

The Bhagavad Gita, translations by Eknath Easwaran, Prabhavananda and Christopher Isherwood, S. Radhakrishnan. (Many other fine translations/annotations also available.)

The Yoga of Spiritual Devotion: A Modern Translation of the Narada Bhakti Sutras, Prem Prakesh. (A simple, inspiring text on the spiritual path of love and devotion.)

The Yoga Sutras of Patanjali, Edwin F. Bryant. (A 600-page tome that provides a wealth of information on the history, philosophy, and practice of classical yoga. Serious students of yoga will want to read this text as well as Swami Hariharananda Aranya's *Yoga Philosophy of Patanjali*.)

Yoga Philosophy of Patanjali, Swami Hariharananda Aranya. (A unique and profound account of classical yoga by a scholar-monk.)

Recommended

Be Here Now, Baba Ram Dass. (Classic introductory book on Eastern philosophy. An easy and entertaining read.)

How to Know God, Prabhavananda and Isherwood. (Best introduction to the yoga philosophy of Patanjali.)

The Essential Swami Ramdas, Swami Ramdas. (Inspiring writings of a great twentieth-century *bhakti* yogi.)

The Gospel of Sri Ramakrishna, Swami Nikhilananda. (A revered *bhakti* classic.)

The Synthesis of Yoga, Sri Aurobindo. (Profound essays on yoga by Sri Aurobindo, the renowned twentieth-century Indian guru-philosopher. If you appreciate this book and crave more Aurobindo, get a copy of *The Life Divine*.)

The Upanishads, translations by Mascara, and by Prabhavananda and Isherwood. (Other fine translations also available.)

The Yoga Tradition, Georg Feuerstein. (Outstanding reference book on the history, literature, philosophy, and practice of yoga.)

Kashmir Shaivism

<u>Highly Recommended</u>

Pratyabhijnahrdayam: The Secret of Self-Recognition, Jaideva Singh. (The basic introductory handbook to the abstruse philosophical system of recognition. Not for the intellectually challenged. *The Doctrine of Recognition*, out of print but available as an ebook, is, thanks to the editing of Paul Muller-Ortega, the best version of this text.)

Siva Sutras: The Yoga of Supreme Identity, Jaideva Singh. (The foundational text of Kashmir Shaivism.)

The Doctrine of Vibration, Mark S.G. Dyczkowski. (A scholarly analysis of the doctrines and practices of Kashmir Shaivism.)

The Philosophy of Sadhana, Deba Brata SenSharma. (Outstanding text that deals clearly and extensively with the ultra-important topic of *Shaktipat*, the Descent of Divine Power, or Grace. Must-reading for serious mystics.)

The Triadic Heart of Siva, Paul Eduardo Muller-Ortega. (An ultra-esoteric text about the Heart [*Hridaya*] as Ultimate Reality, Emissional Power, and Embodied Cosmos.)

<u>Recommended</u>

Camatkara: The Hidden Path, Igor Kufayev. (A unique and interesting consideration of Tantric Shaivism.)

Kundalini, The Energy of the Depths, Lilian Silburn. (As an Amazon.com reviewer puts it, "The foremost modern exposition of Kundalini.")

Spanda Karikas: The Divine Creative Pulsation, Jaideva Singh. (An elaboration of the dynamic aspect of Transcendental Consciousness.)

Miscellaneous

<u>Highly Recommended</u>

Beyond the Power of Now: A Guide to, and Beyond, Eckhart Tolles Teachings, L. Ron Gardner.

Introduction to Objectivist Epistemology, Ayn Rand. (Must-reading for all mystics.)

Objectivism: The Philosophy of Ayn Rand, Leonard Peikoff. (Must-reading for all mystics.)

The Ayn Rand Lexicon, Ayn Rand. (If you read only one Ayn Rand book, make it this one.)

The First and Last Freedom, J. Krishnamurti. (Must-reading for all mystics. If you appreciate this book and want to read more Krishnamurti, get his multivolume *Commentaries on Living*.)

The Way of Chuang Tzu, Thomas Merton. (Other translations also available.)

<u>Recommended</u>

A Brief History of Everything, Ken Wilber. (If you're interested in "integral thinking," you'll enjoy this book. If you appreciate it, get *Sex, Ecology, Spirituality: The Spirit of Evolution*.)

Alan Oken's Complete Astrology, Alan Oken. (Best overall book on astrology.)

Ayurveda: The Science of Self-Healing, Vasant Lad. (Fascinating and enlightening exposition of the principles and practical applications of Indian Ayurveda, the oldest healing system in the world.)

Awaken Healing Energy Through the Tao, Mantak Chia. (Classic introductory handbook to the practice and principles of Taoist energy-yoga.)

The Mystique of Enlightenment: The Radical Ideas of U.G. Krishnamurti, U.G. Krishnamurti. (U.G. was the ultimate spiritual iconoclast. Jean Klein called him "pathological." I call him "a great read.")

The Perennial Philosophy, Aldous Huxley. (Classic text by a great writer.)

The Tao Te Ching. (Numerous translations available.)

www.ingramcontent.com/pod-product-compliance
Lightning Source LLC
Chambersburg PA
CBHW051208090426
42740CB00021B/3417